JAMES

A Practical Faith

JAMES
A Practical Faith

By

Murray W. Downey

MOODY PRESS

CHICAGO

To
the alumni
of
Canadian Bible College
serving Christ around the world

Library of Congress Catalog Card Number: 72-77959

ISBN: 0-8024-4228-5

Printed in the United States of America

CONTENTS

FOREWORD

It seems fitting that this compendium, distilled from more than thirty years of teaching "the schools of the prophets," should be shared in print for distribution. Both laymen and preachers alike will find illumination and help for their own lives as well as help to share the riches of the book of James with others. The brevity, simplicity, and variety of approaches tend to stimulate the imagination and to breathe new life into old truths. Those who know the author will immediately recognize the relationship of the book of James to the practical Christian living exemplified in the life of the author. May this book be a blessing to many.

SAMUEL J. STOESZ
Academic Dean
Canadian Bible College

PREFACE

This book is different, but need—not novelty—is my reason for writing. The need for practical Christianity is everywhere apparent, and James is painfully practical. Some accuse him of being legalistic, a stranger to grace; and for that reason, they have even excluded this epistle from the canon of the New Testament. In this age of violence, the spirit of lawlessness has, to a certain extent, invaded Evangelicalism with gusts of revolt. Scriptural standards are being questioned, for there are no absolutes, some say. Granted that we all have our taboos, there are, nevertheless, some well-established principles set down in the Scriptures, for truth is eternal.

Our book is divided into four sections. In Part 1, The Book Surveyed, we deal with preliminaries, or what we call the *ABC* and *D*s of the book. This has to do with Authorship, Background, Content, Date, Design, and Destination. This type of introduction to any book of the Bible should be considered a necessary preliminary to a proper understanding of that book.

Part 2, The Book Searched, aims at involvement by asking questions to provoke discussion. This section is designed to help teachers and lay leaders. These questions have been used in adult Sunday school classes with appreciation. In our travels in Latin America in the summer of 1969, my wife and I witnessed a great need for textbooks for lay leaders seeking to pastor churches and wanting to study the Word of God while continuing to support a family.

Part 3, The Book Sermonized, is written to assist preachers in preaching the Word. A series of messages has been prepared with titles for publicity, propositions for clarity, outlines for unity, parallel passages for scriptural solidarity, a précis for simplicity, and an application for relativity. These can be easily adapted.

The purpose of the last section, Part 4, The Book Studied, is to give readers a taste of in-depth Bible study. Some of this work has been done by students in my classes, who, after working together on the Part 1 preliminaries, were asked to select one key word in an assigned passage for the next day's class. With the use of lexicons, dictionaries, concordances, commentaries, grammars, and Greek word studies, the students sought out the meaning and message of that one word. The understanding of such words as *temptation, perfect, sin, soul, faith, mercy,* and *spirit,* can widen the whole horizon of learning with respect to the teaching of the Scriptures. The enthusiasm of the class over these studies may be reflected in the results of their research.

Finally, the book is written to meet a spiritual need. How many Christians face up to every situation in life in a spirit of triumphant faith? James expected his readers to be triumphant, cheerful, prayerful, peaceful, wise, faithful, practical, humble, patient, unselfish, and not self-willed. Practical James brings all of these virtues to our attention in this letter. James knew Jesus very well; and his message reflects not only how Jesus lived, but how we are to live when Christ is living in us.

ACKNOWLEDGMENTS

The presentation of the *ABC* and *D*s, Authorship, Background, Content, Date, Design, and Destination, has been my own personal procedure in introducing each book of the Bible to students in college. I am indebted to many reputable commentators for their opinions in the preparation of Part 1, The Book Surveyed.

The questions in the second section of the book have been used in local adult Bible classes. Their enthusiasm has been an inspiration to broaden the ministry of the question method in Part 2, The Book Searched.

To Dr. Samuel Stoesz, dean of the faculty at our college, I wish to express my deep appreciation for his keen critical analysis of much of the work in Part 3, The Book Sermonized.

To students in classes in homiletics and general epistles at the Canadian Bible College, I am indebted for suggestions and research in the compilation of Part 4, The Book Studied.

To my son, Deane Downey, head of the English department at our college, I am grateful for proofreading the manuscript.

THE BOOK SURVEYED

THE SURVEY METHOD

Before we started school, some of us learned the *ABCs*. Before studying any book in the Bible, it is important to know, if possible, something about the Authorship of the book, the Background, Content, Date, Design, and Destination of the book. This we call the *ABC* and *D*s.

There are approximately forty human authors for the sixty-six books of the Bible. Each man is different. Each one has his own style, his own point of emphasis, his own purpose in writing. Just as a musician gets a different sound when playing the piano than when playing the pipe organ, so the Holy Spirit has chosen to use many different human instruments. This makes Bible study exciting, to say the least.

In this introductory study of the book of James, we invite our readers to carefully consider this survey of the book. If indeed James was the brother of our Lord, grew up with Him in Nazareth, ate with Him, slept with Him, played with Him, while not knowing exactly just who He was, it opens many windows of light as we read this letter. If he was the pastor of the church at Jerusalem, that was subsequently scattered by persecution, it is easier to understand his solicitude for his flock.

A knowledge of the background is essential to understanding and interpretation. There are several suggestions throughout the epistle, shedding light on the conditions prevalent among the first readers. Then a bird's-eye view of the content of the book is important. In the section on content, we have attempted to outline the book according to subject mat-

15

ter. There was no strain after alliteration. It just seemed to
be there already.

While dating is a delicate subject, in more ways than one,
an early date seems most likely for the book of James. Any
preliminary study of any book in the Bible, should raise the
question, "Why was it written?" The subject of this book's
destination seems quite important, in view of so much current teaching on the identity of the twelve tribes and particularly on the identity of the so-called lost ten tribes.

In all, we consider the study of the *ABC* and *D*s for this
book, or any book of the Bible, to be very important.

AUTHORSHIP

The author of the book of James presents himself as "James,
a servant of God and of the Lord Jesus Christ." Several suggestions have been submitted by commentators as to the
identity of the author. Here now is a list of the James' mentioned in the New Testament:

1. Brother of John, a son of Zebedee and Salome; put to
death by Herod, ca. A.D. 44 (Ac 12:2)
2. Brother of the Lord (Mt 13:55; Mk 6:3; Gal 1:19)
3. Son of Mary (Mt 27:56; Lk 24:10)
4. The less (Mk 15:40)
5. Son of Alphaeus (Mt 10:3; Mk 3:18; Lk 6:15; Ac 1:13)
6. Father of Jude (Lk 6:16; Ac 1:13. The ellipsis in the
expression, *'Ioudan 'Iakōbou*, is rightly supplied in the English Revised Version, "Judas the son of James," not as the
King James Version's "brother.")
7. Leader of the church (Ac 12:17; 15:13; 21:18; 1 Co
15:7; Gal 2:9, 12)
8. Brother of Jude (Jude 1)
9. Servant of God and of the Lord Jesus Christ (Ja 1:1)

Of these nine, number two and seven are the same (cf.
Gal 1:19 with 2:9, 12). Three, five, and maybe six seem to

be identified with two and seven. By this process of identification, the list is reduced to three:

1. Son of Zebedee
2. Son of Alphaeus, one of the twelve
3. Brother of the Lord

The pith of the problem is this: Can we identify two and three? On this question, scholars are divided. We shall ask our readers to consider both viewpoints. Is James the brother of the Lord, identical with James the son of Alphaeus? Or, are they two distinct persons?

First of all, let us consider the reasons given for regarding James the son of Alphaeus as identical with James the brother of the Lord.

1. The book of Acts identifies two people by this name in 1:13 and 12:2: James the son of Alphaeus, and James the son of Zebedee, respectively. We know that each one was an apostle, one of the twelve (Mt 10:2-3). James, the son of Zebedee is eliminated by martyrdom, according to Acts 12:2, in ca. A.D. 44. If the James, mentioned subsequently in Acts 12:17, 15:13, and 21:18, is someone other than James the son of Alphaeus, then it means that this latter apostle disappears from the New Testament after Acts 1:13 and his place is taken by another "James" whose relationship is not specified in the Acts.

2. Let us look at John 19:25. "Now there stood by the cross of Jesus his mother, and his mother's sister, Mary the wife of Cleophas, and Mary Magdalene." Does this verse mention four women or three? Much of the controversy swings on this hinge, and the hinge really squeaks if you become dogmatic one way or the other. To proceed with the argument that the son of Alphaeus is James the brother of the Lord, the verse is read to mean that there are three women mentioned, that His mother's sister is Mary, the wife of Cleophas. Those who hold this view tell us that the names Cleophas and Alphaeus are identical. This would mean that

James the son of Mary and Alphaeus, was a first cousin of
Jesus, whose mother, Mary, was a sister to Mary the mother
of James. And since, they claim, there is no Greek word for
"cousin," then the Greek word for "brother" must be assumed
to mean "cousin." Therefore, they conclude that James, the
son of Alphaeus, is James the Lord's "brother."

It is the author's opinion that James the son of Alphaeus,
is not to be identified with James the Lord's brother, for
several reasons.

1. It seems unlikely that there would be two sisters by
the same name—"Mary." John 19:25 speaks of four women,
not three.

2. We are expressly told in John 7:5 that Christ's brethren
did not believe in Him. This could not apply to James the
son of Alphaeus, who was already an apostle.

3. Accepting James the brother of the Lord, as distinct
from James the son of Alphaeus, makes it unnecessary to
bend the meaning of "brother" to mean "cousin."

4. There are other apostles not mentioned after Acts 1:13,
so that no further mention of James the son of Alphaeus,
presents no problem.

5. To say that it is unlikely that James, the Lord's brother,
would rise to such eminence in the church at Jerusalem
when he was not converted till after the resurrection of
Christ, is a shaky surmise. Peter preached powerfully when
filled with the Holy Ghost just three years after his conversion. It must have been at least ten years before James rose
to a place of leadership in the church of Jerusalem.

6. James the son of Alphaeus was never a spokesman or a
leader according to the records in the gospels. But the James
of Acts 15 presided over the Council of Jerusalem with promi-
nent apostles present.

7. The twelve apostles were eventually scattered from
Jerusalem (Mk 16:15, 20; Ac 1:8). But the James of Acts
12:17, 15:13, 21:18; and Galatians 1:19, 2:9 was a pillar, a

bulwark, a tree planted, a bishop, a pastor who continued in the capital until he was martyred in ca. A.D. 62.

8. Some see a similarity in the greetings sent by James to the churches after the Jerusalem Council in A.D. 49 (Ac 15:23), to the greeting in James 1:1.

The James, who stands up to say, "My sentence is . . ." (Ac 15:19) is in considerable contrast to James the son of Alphaeus, the apostle in the gospel records. We have no record of his ever having expressed a personal opinion about anything. James the Lord's brother was a leader, a spokesman, a consultant, and was respected as such by Paul and the other apostles.

The author of this epistle was referred to as "Camel-knees." As a result of so much time spent on his knees in prayer, calluses had formed. This fits in perfectly with the sentiment of James' epistle, for the letter abounds in references to prayer. The preacher practiced what he preached.

James is also called "the Just" because of his exceeding righteousness. Thus he could speak with authority when he wrote, "The effectual, fervent prayer of a righteous man availeth much." The letter sets forth a high standard of righteous conduct—almost, some think, to a point of legality. This impression, however, may be the result of letting our standards sink to such a low level that lawlessness is regarded as both proper and popular. The "law of liberty" and the "law of the Spirit of life in Christ Jesus" are never to be interpreted as freedom to sin. Jesus said, "Whosoever committeth sin is the bondservant of sin" (Jn 8:34).

The church Fathers also spoke of the author of this epistle as "Oblias," meaning "bulwark of the people." This agrees with the reference in Galatians 2:9, where Paul refers to James as one of the "pillars" of the church at Jerusalem. It seems that he may have had even more prominence in that church than either Peter or John. When the other apostles ran into stormy seas in their discussion of issues that threat-

ened the unity of the apostolic church in Acts 15, it was
James who calmed the troubled waters with his words of
wisdom. This was not the only time that he was needed to
still the seas of sinful strife among the brethren (Ja 4). He
is mentioned before Peter and John in Galatians 2:9.

Josephus says that James was stoned to death by order of
Ananias. Eusebius says he was thrown down from the pin-
nacle of the temple and then beaten to death with a club.
Hayes, an historian, says it was believed by both Christians
and Jews that the afflictions that came upon Jerusalem in
A.D. 70 were as a judgment on the city for its treatment of
James. It would seem more likely, however, that the judgment that fell on Jerusalem, foreseen and foretold by Christ,
came when the Jews' cup of iniquity was full; when they had,
as a nation, killed the prophets, crucified their Messiah, and
then proceeded to accord the same treatment to the apostles
and the church.

Therefore, it would seem that James lived and died in
Jerusalem. Having met many Jews that came to Jerusalem
to observe Jewish festivals, and having ministered to the
many thousands converted to Christ through the early
preaching of the apostles, he wrote to his Jewish brethren,
the twelve tribes, scattered abroad (Ja 1:1). As former pastor, he would feel deep concern for his flock. While the
apostles went everywhere preaching the Word (Mk 16:20),
James remained in old Jerusalem, until his soul was translated to the New Jerusalem above.

In summary, the certain identity of the James who is the
author of this epistle, is not conclusive. Of the two apostles
by this name, James the son of Zebedee, and James the son
of Alphaeus, neither one seems to fit. The former was martyred early; the latter was not a leader. The possibility of
James the son of Alphaeus, being identical with James the
brother of the Lord, is ruled out by the statement in John 7:5
concerning the unbelief of His brethren. An apostle would

scarcely be classed as an unbeliever. From Galatians, we learn that James the brother of the Lord, was a pillar in the Jerusalem church. This coincides with the prominence of the James at the Council of Jerusalem in Acts 15 and the subsequent eminence of the James in Acts 21:18. This James was singled out for special attention after the resurrection, where he is distinguished from the twelve in 1 Corinthians 15 and Acts 1. Thus, it seems that James the brother of the Lord, is the author.

The acceptance of this possibility (that James the brother of the Lord, is the author) throws much light on the home-life of Joseph and Mary in Nazareth. The suggestion is worth a thesis. While Joseph and Mary knew who Jesus was, His brethren did not. This misunderstanding brought both good and evil to the fore. It was a poor home (there are many allusions to this poverty in the epistle); but nevertheless, there were hospitality, generosity, good neighbor relations. Likely, there was much wrangling but there was also the quiet, gentle, impartial, and unhypocritical testimony of Jesus and His parents. This godly influence did not break through the thick barrier of unbelief till after Christ had risen. The Scriptures were studied but not understood by some members of that household. There were many trials but as many triumphs. There was sickness in the home, but there were healings too; and the family learned that God answers prayer.

The above hypothesis may sound somewhat speculative. Joel predicted, "Your old men shall dream dreams" (2:28)! At any rate, if true, it would provide an interesting study for the background for James' ministry and message. James was well schooled for his steadfast endurance as pastor in the religious capital of the world. The consistent testimony of a brother who was different, the radiant witness of a mother who really knew God, the godly example of a faithful father who loved the Scriptures and taught them to his children, must have made a profound impression on James. This influence finally paid off. This should be an encouragement to godly parents and to any godly son or daughter, waiting for that day when all the family will be in the shelter of the fold.

The twentieth-century student must study the content of this treatise in the light of its first-century setting. The early converts to Christ and His church were converted out of Judaism. In an upper room in Jerusalem, one hundred and twenty disciples gathered to pray and to wait for the promised Comforter (Ac 1:4, 14-15). The Comforter came (2:2-4). The promise of the Father was fulfilled. The risen and exalted Saviour had been glorified; and in accordance with His promise, the Holy Ghost had come to dwell in and among His people forever (John 7:38-39, 14:16; Ac 2:33). His coming was attested by many miracles—the mighty wind, the cloven tongues of fire, the speaking in tongues, and the conversion of about three thousand Jews gathered at Jerusalem "out of every nation under heaven" (Ac 2:5).

The coming of the Comforter was followed by a revival in Jerusalem that swept multitudes of Jews into the kingdom of God. At first disciples were added (Ac 1:13-14), then multiplied (6:1), then greatly multiplied (6:7), until Jerusalem was filled with the new doctrine (5:28) of a crucified, risen, and exalted Saviour (10:37-42). The Jewish Sanhedrin could not stomach such success. They flew to the colors to conserve their religion from extinction. They threatened, imprisoned, flogged, and persecuted. They endeavored to kill Paul, the Christian convert who had once been one of their ringleaders. Before his conversion, Saul of Tarsus, full of religious wrath, had led his fellowmen in a crusade designed to exterminate the new faith (9:1). He was arrested by the sovereign Saviour, convicted for his being on the wrong course, and thoroughly converted to the Lord Jesus Christ. The machinations of hell could not prevail against the church. The infant church grew until it became a thriving adult, circling the globe with the redemptive message.

When Paul reported to James the success of his missionary ministries among the Gentiles, James, the bishop of the church at Jerusalem, responded, "Thou seest, brother, how many thousands of Jews there are which believe; and they are all zealous of the law" (Ac 21:20). These converted Jews, unlike their Gentile brethren, were "all zealous of the law." This can be understood when their Jewish background is considered. It is very doubtful if anyone is at once freed at conversion from all the religious trappings of the culture in which he was bred. Paul, wishing to be "made all things to all men" (1 Co 9:19-22), conformed to the cultural pattern proposed by James (Ac 21:21-27); but the record reveals that it did not help much. Other Jews, yet unconverted to Christ, stirred up a riot, and Paul escaped by the skin of his teeth.

James succeeded Peter as the outspoken leader of the Jewish church at Jerusalem, which had many thousands in its membership. It had become a strong church, producing men like Barnabas (Ac 11:22), who went to Antioch to assist in the revival there and to do some follow-up work.

Barnabas sought Saul who had returned to his hometown at Tarsus, and together they helped to established a strong, missionary church at Syrian Antioch. This became the radiating center for Paul's future missionary endeavors. As witnesses went everywhere from Jerusalem preaching the Word (Ac 8:4), Satan became enraged. The apostles were at first lodged at Jerusalem (8:1). Many believers were scattered (8:4). Providentially, the apostles were dislodged (cf. Mk 16:15, 20; Ac 1:8). Testimony reaches us through the writings of the church Fathers that before leaving the sacred city, the apostles asked James, the brother of the Lord, to remain and weather the storm. James, mentioned by Paul as one of the "pillars" of the Jerusalem church, conceded. He, Oblias ("bulwark of the people"), refused to quit. He wrestled through in prayer till victory was won. His congregation was scattered. Reports reached him of their trials, temptations, talk, and desperate need for counsel and encouragement. He wrote to help them. Their faith was being sorely tested; they were meeting to worship (Ja 2:2), but too often they were hearing without heeding (1:22). They had "high talk" and "low walk" (Ja 2). Their tongues were on the loose (Ja 3). Believers had become quarrelsome, arrogant, and worldly-minded (Ja 4). They had become fraudulent in their business dealings, with the rich getting richer and the poor poorer (Ja 5). It is easy to see that a letter needed to be written to encourage a return to steadfast endurance, pure religion, brotherly affection, practical faith, bridled speech, Christian compatibility, sanctified service, humility, harmony in human relationship, and patient endurance of injustice and human infirmity.

The book of James, then, has a very definite Jewish background. The place of worship is the synagogue (2:2). The Jewish creed, the *Sh'ma Israel*, that God is one, is accepted (2:19). The oaths prohibited are Jewish (5:12). The sins denounced are those to which Jews were addicted—pride, conceit, ostentation, being overbearing, and fraud.

Though the book has a Jewish background, its message is universal. In the matter of sin, there is no difference between Jew and Gentile, between rich and poor, old and young, black or white, educated or illiterate. All have sinned. All have come short. All are guilty before God. There is no help, no hope apart from Christ, the almighty Saviour. He has broken down all the barriers at Calvary. By the blood of His atonement, all believers have been made one in Christ Jesus.

Unless this divided world returns to *Him*, the barrier-breaker, generation gaps, race riots, revolutions, wars, and violence will increase. In the meantime, the whole church

of Christ is admonished to be patient until the coming of
Christ to right all wrongs (Ja 5:9).

I. The saint and the storm, 1:1-12
   A. Introduction, v. 1
   B. Reasons why saint has victory through storm, vv.
   2-12
      1. Inward joy not dependent on outward circum-
      stances, v. 2
      2. Purposes of trials, vv. 3-12
         a) Develop faith, v. 3
         b) Teach patience, v. 4a
         c) Perfect character, v. 4b
         d) Encourage to pray, v. 5
         e) Lead to steadfastness, vv. 6-8
         f) Help us find true riches, vv. 9-11
         g) Make us candidates for crown of life, v. 12

II. The saint and sin, 1:13-17
   A. God not responsible for temptation, v. 13
   B. Source of sin is one's own lust, v. 14
   C. Wages of sin is death, v. 15
   D. Nothing but good comes from immutable God, vv.
   16-17

III. The saint and the Scriptures, 1:18-27
   A. The saint begotten (or born again) through Word,
   v. 18
   B. Exhortation to hear the Word, v. 19
   C. Exhortation to be slow to speak, vv. 19-21
   D. Reasons for obedience to Word
      1. That to hear and not heed is to be deceived,
      v. 22
      2. That to forget what God has spoken is reprehen-
      sible, vv. 23-24

3. That only in obedience to the Word is there
   blessing, v. 25
4. That religion without obedience is vanity, vv.
   26-27

IV. The saint and snobbery, 2:1-13
   A. Respecting the rich to elevate one's personal pres-
      tige incompatible with faith in Jesus Christ, v. 1
   B. Illustration of snobbery, vv. 2-3
   C. Because motive behind such action is evil, v. 4
   D. Unreasonableness of such treatment, vv. 5-7
   E. Christians transgress royal law of love when they
      cater to rich to gain personal advantage, vv. 8-13

V. The saint and service, 2:14-26
   A. Fruitless faith illustrated and applied, vv. 14-20
     1. Doing nothing for destitute brother, vv. 14-17
     2. Demons believe in God but behavior reveals
       character, vv. 19-20
   B. Fruitful faith, vv. 21-26
     1. Abraham, vv. 21-24
     2. Rahab, vv. 25-26

VI. The saint and his speech, 3:1-12
   A. Speech an index to person's character, vv. 1-2
   B. The power of speech illustrated, vv. 3-8
     1. By power of bit to control horse, v. 3
     2. By power of helm to control ship, v. 4
     3. By power of spark to start fierce fire, vv. 5-6
     4. By power of men to control beasts, yet are
       powerless to control tongues, vv. 7-8
   C. Hypocrisy of speech of some professing Christians,
      vv. 9-12

VII. The saint and sagacity, 3:13-18
   A. Marks of true wisdom, vv. 13, 17-18
     1. Good life, v. 13

      2. Meekness, v. 13
      3. Purity, v. 17
      4. Peace, v. 17
      5. Gentleness, v. 17
      6. Compatibility, v. 17
      7. Mercy and good fruits, v. 17
      8. Absence of partiality, v. 17
      9. Absence of hypocrisy, v. 17
   B. Marks of false wisdom, vv. 14-16
      1. Bitterness, v. 14
      2. Envy, v. 14
      3. Strife, v. 14
      4. Corrupt fruit, vv. 14-16

VIII. The saint and supplication, 4:1-12
   A. Hindrances to prayer, vv. 1-6
      1. Strife among brethren, v. 1
      2. Carnality in heart, v. 1
      3. Negligence and carelessness, v. 2
      4. Asking amiss, v. 3
      5. Worldliness, v. 4
      6. Quenching Spirit, v. 5
      7. Paying no attention to Scriptures, v. 5
      8. Pride, v. 6
   B. Way to recovery, vv. 5-12
      1. Obey Spirit as He speaks through Word, v. 5
      2. Humble yourself, receive grace from God, v. 6
      3. Submit to God, v. 7
      4. Resist devil, v. 7
      5. Draw nigh to God, v. 8
      6. Clean up, get right with God and men, quit being a hypocrite, v. 8
      7. Stop joking about sin, be thorough in repentance, v. 9
      8. Recognize God's way up is down, v. 10
      9. Be contrite, not critical of others, v. 11

IX. The saint and self-will, 4:13-17
   A. Illustration of self-will, v. 13
   B. Ignorance of such self-assertion, v. 14
   C. Correction of self-will, vv. 15-17
     1. Will to do God's will, v. 15
     2. It is evil to leave God out of planning, v. 16
     3. Neglecting to heed admonition is sin, v. 17
X. The saint and the second coming of Christ, 5:1-12
   A. Description of last days before Christ returns, vv. 1-6
     1. Conflict between capital and labor, vv. 1-4
       a) Judgment on luxurious living, vv. 1-2
       b) Judgment on hoarding, v. 3
       c) Judgment on fraud, v. 4
       d) Judgment on the oppression of poor by rich, v. 4
     2. Much pleasure-seeking and self-seeking, v. 5
     3. Much killing, antichristian activity, v. 6
   B. Exhortations to saints in light of these conditions, vv. 7-12
     1. Examples of patience, vv. 7-11
       a) The farmer, v. 7
       b) The prophets, v. 10
       c) Job, v. 11
     2. Be at peace with brethren, v. 9
     3. Be a man of your word, v. 12
XI. The saint and sickness, 5:13-20
   A. If your affliction is sickness, v. 13
   B. If you are well, v. 13
   C. If really sick, v. 14
   D. If sin is the cause of the sickness, v. 15
   E. If others besides sick one have faults to confess, vv. 16-17
   F. If encouragement to prayer is needed, vv. 17-18
   G. If sin is corrected, vv. 19-20

DATE

James may be the earliest book of the New Testament to be written. While the church is mentioned and elders are referred to in the last chapter, there is little suggestion of much development in church organization. It may have been written as early as A.D 45, shortly after the scattering that took place after the martyrdom of Stephen (Ac 7:54-60; Ja 1:1). Josephus fixes the death of James between the death of Festus and the arrival of his successor, Albinus (i.e., A.D. 62). So, it was probably written after A.D. 45 and before A.D. 62, but exactly which year is uncertain.

DESIGN

Paul has been called "the apostle of faith"; John, "the apostle of love"; Peter, "the apostle of hope"; and James, "the apostle of good works." Actually, James talks much more about faith than he does of works, but with James, as with Paul, works are the fruit of faith. Faith works. If it doesn't work, it is vain, dead, useless (1 Co 15:2; Ja 2:14-26).

The design of this letter was to encourage and to exhort the saints who had been scattered through persecution, to be triumphant in their trials, steadfast in their faith, practical in their love, careful in their speech, prayerful over their problems, victorious in every circumstance. They are exhorted to be humble, submissive, patient, persevering, merry hearted. They are enjoined "not to pout, nor spout." They are expected to put legs on their faith and a bridle on their tongue. In other words, says James, if you do not practice the Christian faith, it is useless to profess it. Be real!

DESTINATION

The definite destination is not clear. The epistle is addressed to "the twelve tribes which are scattered abroad" (1:1), called the Diaspora. Some consider the ten tribes of Israel to have been lost after their Assyrian captivity in 722

B.C.; then they lost their national identity and became "British Israel." We consider their reasonings to be fanciful, unscriptural, and unhistorical.

Before the Israelites' captivity there was much mingling with Judah (2 Ch 11:13-17, 15:9, 34:6-9). After the Babylonian captivity, there are many allusions to "the twelve tribes" in Ezra, Nehemiah, and Esther. Ezra speaks of the remnant as "Jews" eight times and as "Israelites" forty times (e.g., Ezra 1:3, 2:70, 3:1, 4:12, 7:15, 8:35). Nehemiah records eleven times that they were "Jews" and proceeds to describe them as "Israel" twenty-two times (e.g., Neh 1:6-9, 7:7). The book of Esther, speaking of the same people scattered throughout the Persian world, calls them "Jews" forty-five times. Christ commissioned the twelve to go to none but the lost sheep of the house of Israel (Mt 10:6).

If the term "Jews" was used only of the tribe of Judah and applied to those who returned to Judah after the Babylonian captivity, then it is strange that in the commission given at that time, the twelve confined their ministry to Palestine. If to be a Jew means to be of the tribe of Judah only, then we must consider that Paul was mistaken when he called himself a Jew (Ac 21:39, 22:3) because he was of the tribe of Benjamin (Phil 3:5). He also spoke of himself as an Israelite (Ro 11:1; 2 Co 11:22). The names "Jew" and "Israelite" became synonymous during the exile (Est 3:4). The New Testament uses the word "Jew" 174 times and "Israel" seventy-four times. We use the term to mean "Israelite." James wrote this letter to the twelve tribes, all known as Jews.

The people addressed in this letter were not likely restricted to those who had been scattered abroad from Jerusalem after the stoning of Stephen (Ac 8:1-4). There were Jews from several countries present on the day of Pentecost, "devout men, out of every nation under heaven" (Ac 2:5). About three thousand of these repented, were baptized, and received remission of sins and the Holy Ghost on that day. These were Jews of the Diaspora. These likely carried the gospel back to their own country, but they had had little grounding in the Christian faith. Furthermore, we know that very early in the church outreach, the gospel went to all Judea, to Samaria, and out to the uttermost part of the world (Ac 9:2; 11:19-20; Col 1:23).

The letter was written to displaced persons. They had been scattered like seed cast into the ground to die. Jesus taught us that "the good seed are the children of the kingdom" (Mt 13:38). Christ explained that "Except a corn of wheat fall into the ground and die, it abideth alone: but if it die, it bringeth forth much fruit" (Jn 12:24). The sower is the Son of man. He knows that snug saints, all wrapped up in their silken selfishness, cannot reproduce a harvest till they are taken out of their confined church cloisters and scattered. Too many have fallen asleep in their comfortable pew. Christ has commanded His church to go into all the world to preach the gospel. Some have gone. Some have died to sin, to self, to the world. They are producing a harvest.

The letter was addressed to brethren (Ja 1:2, 16; 2:1, 14; 3:1, 10; 5:7, 10, 12, 19). There is no point in telling people who are not brethren to count it nothing but joy when they tumble into trials and tribulations. Brethren are children of God. They are in the family of God through a spiritual birth (1 Jn 3:1-2). They have received the Son of God, who is the Word of God, all that the Word declares Him to be (Jn 1:1-18). Many are trying to act like Christians without being Christians. This is hypocrisy. There is no real ecumenism between people who are not Spirit-born brethren in Christ, and children of God, adopted into the family of God. Brethren are believers. They believe in Jesus Christ as Saviour and as Lord. They believe what He taught without quibbling or questioning. They believe without doubting or demythologizing. They believe in both history and prophecy, in heaven and hell, the law of Moses and the love of God. Christians are not commanded to rejoice in their circumstances. They are commanded to rejoice in the Lord irrespective of their circumstances, and to give thanks always for all things (Eph 5:20; Phil 4:4; 1 Th 5:16). Such an ideal is out of the reach of sinners until they receive the sovereign Saviour who makes all things work together for good to those who love God (Ro 8:28).

Although James' readers were Christian brethren, some were not acting like brethren at all. They sorely needed the exhortation of this letter. Some were snobbish, factious, quarrelsome, impractical, careless and unscrupulous in their language, lovers of pleasure, lovers of money, covetous, idolatrous, and full of other faults. "My brethren, these things ought not so to be" (3:10). Whenever the branches get out of touch with the true Vine, they become fruitless and useless. We as Evangelicals have all but lost our influence for this same reason. James shows us the road to recovery in 4:6-11.

PART 2

THE BOOK SEARCHED

THE DISCUSSION METHOD

Divide a large class into groups of twelve, arranging the seating in a circle or at a table facing one another. Appoint someone responsible to lead the discussion, using the questions in the lesson with the intention of getting everyone in the group involved. He should aim to complete the lesson. Try to avoid having anyone monopolize the time for discussion. The timid should be encouraged to participate.

When there are facilities lacking to accommodate the above arrangement, a teacher may introduce the topic for the day, take about ten minutes for orientation in the lesson, then let the class divide into buzz groups of three or four. Let them take about thirty minutes to discuss among themselves what answers they would give to the questions. The teacher could use the last twenty minutes to pool the results of such discussion, to answer questions, or to discuss problems.

Or, try this. Divide a class into as many groups as there are questions for that particular day. Assign one question to each group. Allow thirty minutes for group discussion, and use the last thirty minutes for class discussion.

In a smaller class, the teacher could assign one question to each one in the class the week before. The questions may be dealt with, giving some time for class discussion after each one has reported on his findings.

Departmentalized Sunday schools have at least one disadvantage. They tend to segregate certain age groups. Barriers are erected between old and young, married and unmarried, children and their parents, professional people and business people. We suggest that for the summer quarter, the discussion groups be mixed to include members from different departments. The so-called generation gap is not a matter of age but of adaptability. It is really a communication gap. This would also be an experience in group dynamics, which could save the school from the usual summer slump. The object of this approach would be to develop better communications between all age levels, from junior high to adult.

Responsibility for leading the discussion should rotate. Assignments of topics should be made well in advance. Encourage full participation.

THE *ABC* AND *D*s

1. What do you learn about James in this epistle?
2. If James the brother of the Lord, is the author, how might this affect him as a person? As a pastor? As an author?
3. To what two James' are we introduced in Acts chapter one? Is any other James alluded to (Ac 1:13-14; Gal 1:19)? In view of the death of one James in Acts 12:2, to which James might the book of Acts refer in 12:17, 15:13-21, and 21:18-25?
4. Would James the Lord's brother, be a full-blood brother? Why? When was he converted (Jn 7:3, 5; Ac 1:13-14)? Was this James an apostle? Was he, then, the man mentioned by Paul in Galatians 1:19? Does the word "apostle" apply only to the twelve (Ac 14:14)?
5. Was James the son of Alphaeus, in Jerusalem after the dispersion that arose after the stoning of Stephen (Ac 8:1-4)? Did the apostles continue in Jerusalem (Mk 16:15, 20)?
6. Do you believe that Mary and Joseph had children born to them after the birth of Christ (Mt 1:24-25, 13:55-56)?
7. Were James' original readers Jews or Gentiles? Chris-

tians or non-Christians? Poor or rich? Check the epistle carefully.

8. Go through the letter and write down as many adjectives as you have time for, descriptive of the condition of these first readers.

9. Consider the ways in which the message of the book of James is relevant to our times. For instance, why do the righteous suffer? Does James deal with the racial issue? Does he give social implications of the gospel? What does he say about war (on all levels)? The rat race to get rich? Capital and labor disputes? Sickness and healing? In this question, merely try to spot the portions which suggest the problems prevalent in the first century. You can discuss these issues later.

10. Name ten important subjects dealt with in this epistle. Outline the epistle to show its main content.

THE SAINT AND THE STORM

James 1:1-12

1. How is James related to Jesus, according to verse one? How is he related to God? What does this relationship suggest about the relationship of God and Jesus Christ?

2. Define what is meant by "temptations" in verse two. Does your definition fit the use of the word as found in such passages as Genesis 22:1, Matthew 6:13, Hebrews 3:8-9, and James 1:13? (See pp. 87-92 on "Temptation.")

3. Of what value are trials?

4. In what ways may trials develop patience? Christian character? Prayer life? Faith?

5. What illustrations does James use in this passage? Explain in each case what he is illustrating.

6. What is a "double minded man" in verse eight, in the light of its context?

7. In what sense is a "brother of low degree" to be considered "exalted" (Eph 1:3-4, 15-23; Ja 2:5)?

8. How do trials make Christians candidates for the crown of life, according to verse twelve? Distinguish between the "crown of life" and "eternal life" in Romans 6:23 (cf. 1 Co 9:25; 1 Th 2:19; 2 Ti 4:8; 1 Pe 5:4; Rev 2:10).

9. Going back over the passage, make a summary of the valuable lessons to be learned and therefore the reasonableness of our counting it all joy whenever we encounter the storms of life.

10. In the light of this passage, discuss the problem of human suffering, especially as it applies to the suffering of the saints (cf. Gen 50:20; Ro 8:28-29; Ja 5:10-11; 1 Pe 4:12-13).

The Saint and Sin

James 1:13-17

1. What is sin, according to the following passages? Romans 14:23; Galatians 5:19-21; James 4:17; and 1 John 3:4, 5:17. (See also pp. 131-34.)

2. Where does sin usually show up first when a Christian is under testing (Gen 3:13; Ps 19:14, 106:33; Ja 1:13)?

3. While God permits evil, is He the author of it (Ro 5:12; Ja 1:14, 17)?

4. What is death (Ro 6:23; Ja 1:15; Rev 21:8)?

5. What successive steps lead to a person's downfall and ultimate death (Ja 1:14-15)?

6. How is the fact that God is immutable (unchangeable) related to Christian stability in a world of such a vast variety of temptations (Heb 6:17-19, 13:5-9; Ja 1:17)?

7. Believers are referred to as "saints" sixty-one times in the New Testament. Are saints subject to temptation (1 Co 1:2, 11; 3:3; 10:13)? How were the saints in the book of James tempted to sin (Ja 1:13-17)?

8. What is wrong with blaming God for the evil in the world (Ja 1:16-17)?
9. Who, then, is to blame for the evil about us (Ro 5:12-21; Ja 1:14)?
10. Briefly state what you understand to be the Bible's teaching on the relationship of a Christian and sin. Base most of your answer on what you see in James 1:13-17.

The Saint and the Scriptures

James 1:18-27

1. Do you see any relationship between this portion, with its emphasis on the Word, and the previous discussion on temptation? Explain. How was the Word of God related to the temptation of Christ recorded in Matthew 4? How is the Word related to our spiritual warfare, according to Ephesians 6:10-18?
2. How is the Word of God related to the new birth, according to James 1:18? Explain the biblical harmony on this theme, as found in John 1:12-13, 3:5; 1 Corinthians 4:15; Titus 3:5; and 1 Peter 1:23.
3. Explain the expression, "That we should be a kind of firstfruits of his creatures" (cf. Ex 13:2, 22:29; Ro 8:23; 1 Co 15:20-23).
4. How is the Word of God related to anger, according to James 1:19-21?
5. Explain what is meant by "the engrafted word" in James 1:21? How does the word *meekness* fit into this context? Why are even the "beloved brethren" (Ja 1:16) in need of the exhortation in James 1:21, with a view to saving their souls? (See also pp. 122-26.)
6. Does going to church on Sunday to hear the Word of God preached, terminate your responsibility to the Word the rest of the week, according to James 1:22?
7. How is the Word of God like a mirror (Ja 1:23)? The

mirror reveals dirt but does not remove it. How is sin removed, according to John 1:29, Hebrews 9:14, and 1 John 1:7-9?

8. How does the Word of God become "the perfect law of liberty" (Jn 8:36; Ro 8:2-4; Ja 1:25)? When a person has been redeemed or released from bondage to sin, is the desire to live right imposed upon him or implanted in him? Discuss this. (See also pp. 98-102.)

9. What are the marks of a vain religion according to 1:26-27? Is James *too* practical at this point? How is the social gospel related to the saving gospel?

10. Note the relationship of a saint to the Scriptures in the Psalms (e.g., Ps 1 or 119).

The Saint and Snobbery

James 2:1-13

1. What is snobbery? After getting a dictionary definition, explain it in terms of the illustration used by James in the passage above. Check your definition with the last part of Jude 16. (See also pp. 105-8.)

2. Who is more liable to pay respect to persons for the sake of gaining personal advantage, the rich or the poor? Explain. What is their motive?

3. Do the Scriptures teach that all men are to be treated alike (Ro 12:10, 13:7; 1 Ti 5:17; Heb 13:7, 17)? Explain.

4. In what sense are all men alike (Is 53:6, 64:6; Ro 3:19-23, 5:12, 10:12-13; Col 3:25)? Are there *moral* differences (Mt 23:14-15; 2 Ti 3:13)? What differences divide Christians? Non-Christians?

5. What is "the royal law" of James 2:8? How is "the royal law" related to "the perfect law of liberty" in 1:25 and 2:12?

6. Into what two basic laws did Christ summarize the Ten

Commandments, according to Matthew 22:36-40 (cf. Ro 8:2; Gal 5:22-23)?

7. If we expect to obtain mercy, how should we mellow our judgment of those who do us wrong (Mt 5:7; Ja 2:13; 1 Pe 3:8-14, 4:8; see also pp. 126-28)?

8. Why is "respect to persons," illustrated by James in this passage, to be regarded as committing sin (2:9)?

9. Do you see any relationship between the snobbish treatment of the poor person in this passage and the unwholesome attitudes between persons of different races, religions or denominations?

10. What would you say is the chief source of such snobbishness? What is the cure?

THE SAINT AND SERVICE
James 2:14-26

1. What two examples of dead faith does James give in 2:14-20? (See also pp. 113-17.)

2. What two examples of living faith does James give in 2:21-26?

3. Is anyone saved by his own efforts (Eph 2:8-9; Titus 3:5)? Who then is the Saviour, the only Saviour (Mt 1:21; Ac 4:12, 16:31; Ro 10:13)?

4. Does saving faith result in works (Eph 2:8-10; Titus 3:8)? Is Paul then in conflict with James on the relation between faith and works (cf. Titus 2:11-15; Ja 2:17)? Which must come first?

5. Did Abraham obtain justification by works or by a faith that worked, according to Romans 4:9-12 and Hebrews 11:8-17?

6. Did Rahab have any inherent goodness to plead as ground for her justification? Why? Does anyone else (Is 53:6, 64:6; Jer 17:9; Mt 9:12-13; Ro 3:9-20)?

7. How does the action of Rahab stand in contrast to the actions of others in Jericho, according to the record in Joshua 2? In what ways was her faith expressed?

8. If becoming a Christian involves receiving Someone and believing something, figure out, from these verses, whom and what: Mark 1:14; John 1:12, 3:14-18, 36; Romans 1:16; 1 Corinthians 15:1-4; and 1 John 5:12-13.

9. Does salvation by grace make allowance for continuance in sin (Ro 5:20—6:6)?

10. Suggest some suitable forms of Christian service that you or your class might undertake in your locality.

The Saint and His Speech

James 3:1-12

1. What illustrations of the power of the tongue do you find in this passage? (See also pp. 120-22.)

2. The Greek word for "masters" in verse one is *didaskaloi*, meaning "teachers." Why does James put a restraint on human ambition to be teachers? What responsibility does such an office hold (Mt 12:36-37, 23:14-15; 1 Ti 5:17; Heb 13:7-9; 2 Pe 2:1-3)?

3. How is responsibility for the use of the tongue illustrated by the use of a bit in a horse's mouth?

4. How is responsibility for the use of the tongue illustrated by the use of a rudder in a ship?

5. How is the destructive power of the tongue illustrated in the spread of a fire from one spark?

6. How does human weakness most commonly manifest itself? What are the characteristics of the perfect or the mature man?

7. Look up the references to the tongue in the book of Proverbs. You may use a concordance. List your findings. The reading of Proverbs will widen your information on the importance of your use of language.

8. Why is the tongue more difficult to control than the most ferocious beast (Ja 3:7-8)?
9. What does a foul mouth reveal, according to James 3:2? According to Christ (Mt 7:15-20, 12:34-37)?
10. Why the exhortation in James 3:10, "My brethren, these things ought not so to be"?

The Saint and Sagacity
James 3:13-18

1. What is sagacity? What synonym is used for the word in the passage above? Discuss what you consider to be the essential difference between wisdom and knowledge.
2. What two kinds of wisdom are dealt with in this passage? What are the identifying marks of each?
3. To what extent do you consider much secular education today to be "earthly, sensual, devilish" (Ja 3:15)?
4. What does worldly wisdom alone foster? Look closely at each verse in the passage.
5. Where is true wisdom to be found (1 Co 1:30; Col 2:3; 2 Ti 3:15; Ja 1:5, 3:17)?
6. How does the apostle Paul regard the wisdom of this world, according to 1 Corinthians 1:18-31?
7. Why is there so much spiritual ignorance clouding men's minds in this so-called enlightened age (Ro 1:21-25; 2 Co 4:3-4; Eph 4:17-19; Ja 3:13-15)?
8. Discuss what you consider to be the Christian attitude toward the current trend to obtain one's higher education in institutions that are both unchristian and antichristian.
9. How do you explain the current conditions on many campuses, with respect to this passage?
10. What answers do you find stated or implied by James for the widespread unrest on our college campuses— places ostensibly devoted to the pursuit of wisdom?

THE SAINT AND SUPPLICATION

James 4:1-12

1. Would you say that much of our so-called praying is more of a "farce" than a force? Why? Find the answers from the above text.

2. What lies at the root of all strife, according to 4:1? Define "lusts."

3. Is the essence of worldliness "willfulness," according to verse 4 (cf. Is 48:22, 57:20-21; Gal 5:17; Eph 2:13-17)? What is at the root of all discord, according to verse 4 and these passages?

4. Is strife among the brethren an unheard of thing, a rare occurrence, or is it rather common (Gen 4:8-9, 13:8, 21:8-13, 27:41-45, 37:3-4; Ex 2:11-14; Mt 20:20-28; Ac 15:2)?

5. From the beginning, the devil whose very name, *diabolos*, means "the accuser," has been very busy showing discord among brethren. Is James quite aware of this activity of the devil, in dealing with strife (Ja 4:7)? So, are we fighting the real foe when we fight our fellow-men, men of flesh and blood, according to Ephesians 6:12?

6. What does strife among Christian brethren prove, according to 1 Corinthians 3:1-3, 6:5-8; Philippians 2:1-8; and 1 Peter 5:5-8?

7. Outline the successive steps to be taken to restore peace in a divided church, according to this passage.

8. According to James 4:5, what would appear to be the cause of every feud? How does one begin the process of correcting this problem, in verse 7? How does one go about getting right with God (Ja 4:8)? Is verse 8 referring to repentance? How does Scripture relate to our criticizing one another, in verse 11? Discuss the

need for such measures in your group. Do something
about it.

9. How does pride arrest progress, according to this passage? Under whose condemnation do we fall when we
allow pride to rule in our hearts (Pr 16:18; 1 Ti 3:6)?

10. When are the prayers of a saint effectual, according to
James 5:16?

The Saint and Self-Will
James 4:13-17

1. What illustrations of self-will do you see in this lesson?
2. What may be wrong in our planning ahead, according to
James 4:13-15?
3. When is rejoicing an evil, according to this passage?
4. Explain how Christ's parable in Luke 12:15-21 applies
to this passage.
5. How is James' illustration of the brevity of life in James
4:14 related to the saint and self-will?
6. Discuss how these passages relate to the brevity of life:
Psalm 90:9, 102:3, 11; Proverbs 27:1; James 1:10; and
1 Peter 1:24.
7. In what sense is self-will a terrible evil, according to
these passages: 1 Samuel 15:23; Isaiah 14:12-14, 53:6,
55:7; and Luke 19:14, 27?
8. What makes Jesus different, according to Matthew 3:17;
John 5:30 and 8:29.
9. Regarding our self-will, to what end is God at work in
our hearts today (Ro 12:1-2; Eph 1:4-5; Phil 2:13)?
10. What strong temptation faces God's people with respect
to money, according to James 4:13-14 (cf. Mt 6:19-21;
1 Ti 6:9-11)? In view of this, what counsel and warning is given by Christ and Paul respectively in Matthew
6:33, Luke 12:15, and 1 Timothy 6:11-16?

THE SAINT AND THE SECOND COMING

James 5:1-12

1. What light on economic conditions in the last days do you see in this passage?

2. What does the passage teach about the vanity of ill-gotten gain?

3. What does the accumulation of wealth reveal about the human heart, in the light of surrounding suffering and misery?

4. The expression "Lord of sabaoth" means "Lord of hosts," and it alludes to hosts of angels. To what activity of angels does this refer, from the context? Will any fraud, injustice, or dishonest dealing go unnoticed or unjudged? (In Jude 14-15, "saints" likely refers to "holy ones," which, in the light of other passages, has reference to angels; cf. Dan 7:10; 1 Th 4:16; 2 Th 1:7).

5. If Christ was crucified for righteousness' sake when He was here at His first advent, do saints have any right to expect any different treatment, according to James 5:7-12? Even if they are doing right (Jn 15:18-20, 16:33, 17:14; 1 Pe 3:14; Rev 6:9-11, 12:11, 13:7-10)?

6. What examples of patience do you see in James 5:7-11? What is patience, in the light of these illustrations?

7. What did patience mean to the Old Testament prophets referred to in verse 10 (cf. Mt 23:29-37; Ac 7:52)?

8. Why do the righteous suffer, according to John 15:20-21; 2 Timothy 3:12 and 1 Peter 2:19-25, 4:12-13?

9. What is meant by "the early and latter rain," in verse 7, and what did it mean to a farmer in Israel? How may this apply to the church, with respect to the "early rain" revival that came at Pentecost and to the "latter rain" revival we may fully expect before the Lord returns to gather in that harvest (Joel 2:23, 28-32; Mt 24:14; Ac 2:1-5, 16-21; Rev 7:9, 14)?

10. What plain teaching on the second coming of Christ is stated in these passages: John 14:3; Acts 1:11; Titus 2:13; Hebrews 9:28; and Revelation 1:7? How should the certainty of His coming affect present conduct, according to 1 John 3:1-3?

THE SAINT AND SICKNESS

James 5:13-20

1. What specific instruction does James give to one who is suffering? To one who is cheerful? To one who is sick? (See also pp. 135-41.)
2. When one is sick, whom is he to call for help? Why is he to call more than one elder to pray? What are they to do? What promise is given? (See Ja 5:14-15.)
3. How are faith healing and divine healing related? Who is the divine healer (Ex 15:26; Ps 103:3; Mt 8:16-17; Ac 4:9-10; Heb 11:6)?
4. Does the "prayer of faith," that brings restoration to the sick, have its source in the human heart, in the light of James 1:17; Romans 8:26, 10:17; Galatians 5:22-23; Philippians 1:29? Where then?
5. How is divine healing related to the sovereignty of God, according to 2 Kings 1:2-17; Job 2:7, 42:10; John 11:4; Romans 8:28-29; and James 5:11?
6. Is the committal of sin the reason for sickness in the light of Job 1:1, 22, 2:3, 7, 42:7; John 9:2-3; Philippians 2:26, 30, and James 5:15? If sin should be the cause of the sickness, what promise can be claimed in the sick room (see Ja 5:15; 1 Jn 1:9)?
7. Who are the elders of the church (Titus 1:5-9; 1 Ti 3:1-7)? May their faults constitute a barrier to the healing miracle? Do personality barriers, or doctrinal barriers, or any other discord between brethren, hinder the suc-

cess of the prayer for healing? (Study Ja 5:16-17. A
sick room might become the center of a church revival.)

8. What encouragement is given in James 5:17-18 to believe God for a mighty miracle in the midst of appalling
   need?

9. May a Christian brother be sick unto death because of
   his having swerved from the prescribed course, in the
   light of James 5:19-20 (cf. 1 Co 11:28-30)? How are
   such to be recovered from a premature death (Gal 6:1;
   2 Ti 2:24-26; Ja 5:19-20)?

10. The doctrine of divine healing has been badly abused.
    No one, calling himself a believer, should hesitate to
    accept at face value the promises of God to answer
    prayer. Does it seem right to exclude healing from such
    promises as these: Jeremiah 33:3; John 14:13-14, 15:7?

PART 3

THE BOOK SERMONIZED

THE HOMILETICAL METHOD

The homiletical method is designed to assist preachers in their preparation of messages for the ministry of the Word. To help combine theory and practice, this method has been used with students in homiletics courses.

The *proposition* is the sermon in a nutshell. A good sermon can be stated in a single simple sentence. Some preachers set out for Canaan and keep the congregation wandering in the wilderness, wondering where they are being led. If the preacher can stay on the main route, he might find his flock more inclined to follow. It is better to score one goal than to have the congregation register a shutout.

For each sermon, a *key word* has been chosen. The key word is always a plural noun. The key word keeps the major divisions coherent with the proposition. When accurately chosen, it gives the sermon unity, harmony, and clarity.

The *plan* (transitional sentence) is the sermon outlined in harmony with the proposition. A properly prepared sermon will have logical and psychological sequence, and it will have unity. The Word of God reveals the designing of God. Study of the Scriptures will soon convince the sensitive soul that the divine Architect had an overall plan. Although we may err in our apprehension of that plan, it is an exciting and exhilarating experience to search for the divine design, often hidden to careless and casual seekers and revealed to those who hunger and thirst after God.

The *parallel passages* will help illuminate the passage at hand. The best commentary on the Bible is still the Bible.

However, where necessary, a full concordance should be consulted on the use of a word or phrase that raises a difficulty. In preparation, enough parallel passages should be consulted to assure that the interpretation is in harmony with the teaching of the rest of Scripture. There are no contradictions in the Bible, when properly interpreted.

The *preamble* may well be the introduction to the sermon. It treats the passage from the standpoint of its context. It is the door that opens into the divine sanctuary of truth in the text. And remember that a text out of context is a pretext.

The *précis* is a condensation of the text in plain speech. It is a much fuller presentation of the text than given in the proposition. But it should sufficiently expand the proposition to include the main roads traveled in the text.

The truth is what God says, not what men think. Preach the Word. Preaching is applying the truth of God's Word to human need. The *application* is the sermon applied. A sermon without an application is a waste of time for both pastor and people.

THE SAINT AND THE STORM

James 1:1-12

Title: Why do the righteous suffer?

Text: "Blessed is the man that endureth temptation: for when he is tried, he shall receive the crown of life, which the Lord hath promised to them that love him" (1:12).

Proposition: The righteous may benefit from the storm of life.

Key Word: Benefits

Plan: There are many benefits for the righteous, arising out of difficult trials.

I. Trials develop Christian character, vv. 2-4.
   A. They reveal whether our joy is in Christ or in our circumstances, v. 2.

    B. They prove whether our faith is a "force" or a "farce,"
v. 3.

    C. They produce steadfastness, v. 4*a*.

    D. They round out our Christian experience by exposing our defects, v. 4*b*.

  II. Trials deepen our prayer life, vv. 5-8.

    A. They drive us to God for wisdom when we stand at wits'-end corner, v. 5*a*.

    B. They teach us the love and liberality of God and His desire to answer our prayers, v. 5*b*.

    C. They teach us to trust God when we pray, vv. 6-8.

 III. Trials detach us from this present, passing world. vv. 9-12.

    A. They teach us that earthly riches do not last, vv. 9-11.

    B. They make us candidates for the crown of life, v. 12.

Parallel Passages:

1:1—scattered: Mk 14:27; Ac 8:1, 4, 11:19; 1 Pe 1:1

1:2—temptations: Mt 4:1; Ac 20:19; 1 Co 10:13; 2 Pe 2:9

1:3—patience: Lk 21:19; Ro 5:3-4, 15:4-5; Col 1:11; Heb 12:1

1:4—perfect: Eph 4:13; Col 1:28, 4:12; Ja 1:17, 25, 3:2; 1 Jn 4:18

1:5—wisdom: 1 Co 1:30; Eph 1:17; Col 2:3; Ja 3:13, 17; 2 Pe 3:15

1:6—faith (believe): Mt 9:28-29, 21:22; Mk 9:24, 11:24; Ro 4:18; Heb 11:6

1:8—double-minded: Jos 24:15; Ru 1:18; 1 Ki 18:21; Ja 4:8

1:12—crown of life: 1 Co 9:24-25; 1 Th 2:19; 2 Ti 4:8; 1 Pe 5:4; Rev 2:10, 3:11

Preamble:

   James, who calls himself "a servant of God and of the Lord Jesus Christ," wrote this letter to the twelve tribes of Israel. Throughout the epistle he refers to his readers as his breth-

ren. He even employs the tender term, "beloved brethren."
It is our opinion that the author is James, the Lord's brother.
Some differ, and a few are undecided; but there is general
agreement that he was the pastor of the church at Jerusalem,
that church which became a storm center very soon after the
mass conversions at Pentecost. James rode out the storm.
According to tradition, James was put to death at Jerusalem
in about the year A.D. 62. His ministry may have lasted
thirty years.

The early chapters of the book of Acts record the conversion of crowds to Christ. At first, thousands were added; but
soon, disciples were so multiplied that even the computers
lost count. But in history, whenever God poured out His
Spirit in blessing, Satan, the adversary, got red with rage,
counterattacked, and sought to stamp out the fires being kin-
dled in human hearts. There was little hope for any sweet
and smooth ecumenism in Jerusalem. The apostles refused to
cooperate with dead ritualism and religion. Their Christ was
very much alive.

The Sanhedrin could not stomach the signal success of this
new cult. Stephen was stoned. James' congregation was
driven from the city and reduced to eleven members, all of
them apostles. Then the Jews proceeded to get rid of them.
They killed James the son of Zebedee. They put Peter in
prison, fully intending to kill him too, but the Lord delivered
him. Later, the rest of his congregation were scattered as the
prince of the power of the air, in a mighty whirlwind, sought
to exterminate the church. The gates of hell could not prevail. Saul of Tarsus, sent from Jerusalem on a mission to
murder, was converted to Christ on the Damascus road.
Christians went everywhere preaching the Word. In one
generation the gospel was preached to every creature in the
Roman world (Col 1:6, 23).

James, with a pastoral concern for his scattered flock, wrote this letter to invoke the people of his former congregation to continue in the faith. In the text before us, he exhorts them to be joyfully triumphant in their trials and tribulations. The storm without is not to interfere with the peace within.

Précis:

James exhorts his scattered sheep to count it a great privilege to be tried and tested. The trials of life afford us an opportunity to discover how very real God can be to us in any circumstance. Trials develop character, they reveal the imperfections in our faith. Trials should drive us to God in prayer, not to a psychiatrist in despair. The storm is intended to steady us, to help us to make up our mind whether we are going to go forward or backward. Financial testing will help to wean us from the love of this world and woo us to the world that will never pass away. Trials should teach us to live *this* day in the light of *that day.* Our Lord Jesus Christ will award a crown of life to those who have withstood the tests, to each one whose character stands approved on that day.

Application:

Have you hit high and heavy seas since you set sail for your heavenly home? Cheer up! Christ, your Captain, is in control. He charted the course. He will perfect that which concerns you. He wants to conform you to His image. To do this He must lead you out of the cold calm of your own self-complacency and lead you through troubled waters. In those troubled waters, He wants you to learn that He is both present and precious. Trust Him. Trust Him for wisdom, patience, steadfast faith. Let Him be your constant confidence —today, tomorrow, till He comes. Don't let this world hide that world from your vision. Live this day in the light of that day.

A Christian farmer had a weather vane on his barn. On it were inscribed the words, "God is love." An ungodly neighbor said in derision, "So, God's love is as changeable as the wind." The reply given was, "It means to me that God is love no matter which way the wind blows." Is that your attitude? The crown of life will be given to all who keep on loving Him, no matter what way the wind blows.

THE SAINT AND SIN

James 1:13-18

Title: When God Is First, Sin Is Never

Text: "Have done, then, with impurity and every other evil which touches the lives of others, and humbly accept the message that God has sown in your hearts, and which can save your souls" (Ja 1:21, Phillips).

Proposition: The consequences of sin are the result of irresponsible attitudes.

Key Word: Attitudes

Plan: Irresponsible attitudes toward God and self are a sin which deadens our faith.

   I. Sin is an irresponsible attitude toward the goodness of God.
      A. God does not tempt man with evil, as we think, v. 13.
      B. God is the Father of light and never changes in His goodness, v. 17.
      C. God has given us the truth with a design for good, v. 18.
  II. Sin is an irresponsible attitude toward ourselves.
      A. Our weakness is a fact we must reckon with, v. 14.
      B. Our impatience keeps us from listening and acting in dependence on God's faithfulness, vv. 19-20.
      C. Our failure to cleanse ourselves by the Word causes defeat, v. 21.

III. Sin should not have dominion over us if we accept responsible attitudes toward God and our own selves.

Parallel Passages:

1:13—tempted: Ps 106:14; Mk 1:13; 1 Co 10:13
1:14—lust: Ro 1:24; Gal 5:16; 1 Ti 6:9; 2 Ti 2:22, 3:6
1:15—sin: Ps 7:11-16; Pr 21:4, Ja 4:17; 1 Jn 3:4, 5:17
1:15—death: Eze 18:31-32; Ro 5:12, 6:23, 8:6
1:17—above: Jn 8:23, 6:33; Eph 1:20-23; Col 3:1
1:18—begat (born): Jn 1:13, 3:3, 5, 7; 1 Jn 2:29, 3:9, 5:4
1:18—word of truth: Jn 1:1, 14, 6:63, 14:6; 1 Pe 1:23
1:18—firstfruits: Ro 16:5; 1 Co 15:20-23, 16:15

Preamble:

In the previous portion of this chapter, practical James has explained why and how we may count the trials of life as opportunities for triumph. To a Christian, Christ is sovereign in every circumstance. Christ is supreme over all. Christ is in the believer; the believer is in Christ. Nothing reaches our lives without His permission, and He only permits what is best. Therefore we are enjoined, in the opening of this book, to count it all joy whenever we run into stormy seas. To a child of God, it is "not the strength of the gale, but the set of the sail that determines the way he goes." If our sail is set right, we will rejoice when we encounter the stiff winds of trial and testing. Why? Because trials develop Christian character. They deepen our prayer life by teaching us to get rooted in God. They help to detach us from this present world, for when we feel at home here, we tend to become settlers rather than pilgrims. Heaven is our home.

The congregation at Jerusalem had been scattered. Were such circumstances ground for regret? A reason for recession? Never! God uses the winds of adversity to deepen our roots in His love. He makes His children candidates for the crown of life. We are a royal priesthood (1 Pe 2:9). As such, we are expected to share in the conquest of Christ over evil.

Christians are not promised smooth sailing, but they are promised a safe landing. Their ship is seaworthy and can stand the tempest, the strain, the gusts, the gale. Our Pilot is the Sovereign of the seas, for He rides upon the storm and makes the wind His chariot.

However, external trials may become internal temptations. Trials may drive us to prayer or they may drive us to despair.

Can a Christian sin? In the refining of silver, some residue will rise to the surface. When blistered by the heat of fiery trial, is it possible that a child of God may lose contact with God? What happens if one continues on a course of sin?

Précis:

When God tests us, we are not to say that God is tempting us to sin. That is to charge God with evil. But if, in the trial, we get out of fellowship with God, we may be easy prey for the enemy. If we allow Satan to drive a wedge between us and God, we soon find we are not self-sufficient. Sin breeds quickly in the heart that is severed from its true source of life. When lust becomes lord, the process of death begins and continues as long as that condition persists.

Sin is not a necessity. Sin is the result of our own deliberate choice to go our own way instead of God's way. God tests us to purify us, to make us like His Son. He was tempted in all points as we are, yet never sinned. God, being holy in His nature, cannot sin. God, being righteous, always does what is right. God is good, always good. There is no variation whatever in His essential nature. As proof of His goodness, we need only consider the fact that He took the initiative in making us His children. We are his firstfruits, having been begotten in His likeness by the Word of truth. As newborn sons, we are called to be conformed to the image of His Son.

Application:

It is wrong and even wicked to blame God for your bad behavior, because sin has its origin in the human heart. The Word of God teaches that man is responsible for his own sin and must repent of his own sin; God does not do our repenting for us. Satan tempts men to sin, but Satan is an external foe. He can only succeed in bringing about our downfall when he can conspire with the fifth columnist within us, our own lust. Lusts are the illegitimate desires that lodge in the confines of our own personality. When we allow an illegitimate desire to drive a wedge between us and our Lord, we are thereby weakened. Living according to our lustful desires, apart from Him, who alone can keep us from falling, we are dead while we live (1 Ti 5:6). Thus aliented from the source of life, we fall prey to Satan's further seductions, and the wages of sin is death.

On the contrary, however, only good proceeds from God. God's character is not subject to any alteration. We can trust in His love and goodness at all times. The fact that He has already communicated His own divine life to us in the new birth is but a token that He will one day present us in His own likeness when He comes to gather His harvest home.

Is sin your problem? Blame no one but yourself. Confess it. Claim cleansing in the precious blood of Christ. Repent. Forsake your sin. Then live in fellowship with the living Christ who has already gained the victory for us over the world, the flesh, and the devil.

What's with you? *You!* Your problem is *you!* Not youth. Not the people you call Puritans. Not your city. Not your community. Not your law enforcement officers. It is your wanting what you want and are determined to have at any cost. The Bible names it sin. And for sin, the pay is death; but the gift of God is eternal life through Jesus Christ our Lord.

THE SAINT AND THE SCRIPTURES

James 1:19-27

Title: Are You for Real?

Text: "Pure religion and undefiled before God and the Father is this, To visit the fatherless and widows in their affliction, and to keep himself unspotted from the world" (1:27).

Proposition: The Word of God enables us to validate our faith.

Key Word: Tests

Plan: James gives two specific tests to help us validate our faith.

I. Use of the tongue
   A. Listening before speaking, v. 19
   B. Being slow to anger, v. 19
   C. Being in control of the tongue, v. 26
II. Obedience to the Word
   A. Hearing and obeying, v. 22
   B. Reading and applying, vv. 22-23
   C. Meditating in and manifesting, vv. 25, 27

Parallel Passages:

1:19—slow to speak: Pr 10:19, 14:17; Mt 17:4-5; Ja 3:1-12
1:20—man's anger: 1 Sa 20:30; Ps 37:8; Pr 15:1, 25:15
1:21—meekness: Mt 11:29; Gal 5:22-23; 2 Ti 2:24-26
1:22—doers of the word: 1 Sa 15:3, 13, 14, 19-23; Heb 11
1:23—hearer of the word: Jn 5:24, 10:27-28; Ro 10:17
1:25—perfect law of liberty: Ro 8:1-3; Gal 3:13, 5:1, 22-23
1:26—religious: Ac 26:5; Phil 3:1-9; Ja 1:27
1:27—world: John 15:18-21, 16:33; Ja 4:4; 1 Jn 2:15-17

Preamble:

We have learned in the first twelve verses of this chapter

that the divine ideal for Christian conduct is that one should rejoice in the midst of tribulation. The reasons are given, then the writer goes on to explain that trials may become temptations. If anyone allows his own lust to drive a wedge between him and his God, then a soul, separated from the Source of life, like a leaf detached from the twig of a tree, will wither and die. To walk in constant communion with God is both the believer's privilege and responsibility.

In the last portion of this chapter, there are several references to the Word. How is the Word related to the subject of temptation and trial? We know that the Scriptures were very intimately related to Christ when He was tempted. It was this sure support that steadied the Son of man when Satan assailed Him during those forty days in the wilderness. This, too, is the basis upon which we must live and act in our conflict with evil. The difference between false religion and real religion lies right here. Real religion rests upon divine dictum. The sword of the Spirit is the Word of God. Carnal weapons are of no avail in this conflict. But we must not only have the Word, we must use it; we must obey it; we must apply it, we must live it. The incarnate Word used the written Word. We have both.

Précis:

Endless confusion results when men try to promote religion and rely more on their "think-so" than they do on God's "say-so." The Word of God has a staying power as well as a saving power. A gentle spirit prevails when heads and hearts bend before the authority of the inspired Scriptures.

Obedience to the Word of God is imperative. The one who knows the Word, but does not keep it, is deluded. He is impractical. He is like a man who looks into a mirror to check on his appearance. He sees dirt but refuses to wash. The man who gets God's Word planted in his heart is free. His conduct proceeds from within so that he acts in harmony with truth and reality. As wings are no burden to a bird, so the good life is native to the new nature God has planted within us. We are free to live the good life when set free from the bondage of sin.

Application:

Real religion proceeds from God. It has come to us through the written Word of God. That written Word directs us to the living Word of God, Christ, who came to this world in exact fulfillment of the Scriptures. Real religion is exceedingly practical. It brings you into right relationship with God through Christ. This in turn issues in a life of service to others. It is vanity to profess a faith you do not possess. We are responsible to show by lip and life that we are in touch with reality.

Since God has spoken to us in His Son, who is the truth, there is no need for religious confusion. Confusion comes only when men are quick to speak their own words and slow to listen to God's Word.

Do you hear and heed God's Word? Do you make a mountain out of a molehill on some small issue? Do you use a minor problem as an excuse for refusing to get right on some major issue? When you begin to obey God in the matters that you do understand, you will soon have light on the matters you do not understand.

THE SAINT AND SNOBBERY
James 2:1-13

Title: A Snob for an Usher

Text: "Don't ever attempt, my brothers, to combine snobbery with faith in our glorious Lord Jesus Christ! But once you allow any invidious distinctions to creep in, you are sinning" (2:1, 9, Phillips).

The Book Sermonized   63

Proposition: The practice of snobbery is inconsistent with faith in Christ.

Key Word: Reasons

Plan: Snobbery is inconsistent with faith in Christ for two reasons.

I. Snobbery is unchristian, not being combined with faith in Christ, v. 1.
   A. All believers in Christ are brothers, v. 1 (cf. Heb 2:11).
   B. All believers in Christ belong to one body, v. 1 (cf. Jn 17:20-21; 1 Co 12:13).
   C. Christ, our glorious Lord, is impartial, v. 1.
II. Snobbery is associated with ungodliness, vv. 2-13.
   A. God is no respecter of persons (Ac 10:34).
      1. He does not judge men by outward appearance, but we do, vv. 2-4 (cf. 1 Sa 16:7).
      2. He has chosen the poor, but we despise them, vv. 5-7.
   B. God is love (1 Jn 4:8).
      1. The law of love governs the members of God's kingdom, v. 8.
      2. The love of God enables us to love our neighbors, v. 8.
      3. The love of God frees us to observe His commandments, vv. 9-12.

Parallel Passages:

2:1—respect of persons: Lev 19:15; Deu 1:17; Jude 16
2:4—judges: Pr 31:9; Is 11:3; Mt 7:1-2; Jn 7:24
2:6—the rich: Lk 21:1-4; Ja 1:10-11, 5:1; Rev 6:15
2:8—the royal law: Jn 3:3, 5, 7; Col 1:13; 1 Pe 2:9; Rev 1:6
2:10—the whole law: Mt 5:19; Gal 3:10, 13, 5:22-23
2:12—law of liberty: Jn 8:32-34; Ro 8:2-3; Gal 5:1
2:13—mercy: Ps 32:10, 145:8; Mt 5:7; Ja 5:11

Preamble:

The dictionary defines a snob as "a person who attaches great importance to wealth, social position, etc., having contempt for and keeping aloof from those he considers his inferiors, often admiring, imitating, and seeking to associate with those whom he considers his superiors." Our text illustrates what snobbery is and then calls the action "sin."

James paints a picture of a proud person, with his head high in the air, strutting into the synagogue, dressed in a splendid suit, with costly jewelry adorning his person. The ushers compete to reach him and to show him to the best seat. Almost immediately a poor man, shabbily dressed, enters the sanctuary. He stands there for a while, apparently unnoticed. After a few scornful glances from both ushers and congregation, the man is asked to sit on a stool in a corner where he would be the least likely to be noticed. Why did the ushers snub one man and kowtow to the other? Why did they discriminate? James projects their thoughts onto the screen; the ushers were guilty of snobbery.

Christians today are in a frantic race to show off. We put the rich and influential on our church boards and mission boards, not because of their spiritual fitness, but because of their social standing. We judge men by their outward appearance; we pay little attention to their intrinsic worth. When we cater to the rich in order to promote our personal prestige, we are sinning, says practical James.

Précis:

Believing brothers, within the family of God, professing faith in Christ as Saviour, and anticipating life in the glory, are not to be found guilty of the sin of snobbery. A man's clothing may not be an index of his character. The man makes the clothes; clothes do not make the man. God is concerned primarily about our character. When the character is right, the outward appearance will adjust accordingly. Some well-dressed people are clothed in the filthy rags of their own religious pride and self-righteousness.

The gospel is a great leveler. God exalts the poor of this world, rich in faith, and gives them a place in His royal family. The rich man must humble himself to the point of being a beggar, begging for mercy, pleading for deliverance, asking God to save him for Christ's sake alone. Such are likewise admitted into the kingdom of God; but like Nicodemus, they must begin at spiritual babyhood, then grow in grace and in the likeness of Christ.

Application:

Do you cater to the rich in the hope of gaining some personal advantage? Are you friendly to folk with social status, simply because you are thereby elevating your personal prestige? Do you snub the poor? Do you scorn the outcast? Do you belong to a "holier-than-thou" church club? And you call that Christianity? Such self-centered saintliness is positive proof that Jesus Christ is indeed "the Stranger of Galilee" to you.

Snobbery is transgression of the law of love. Love is the rule that governs conduct in the royal family. Do you belong to that family? It is unlikely that you love God if you do not love His children. If you are not His child, you may be born into God's family this very hour. How? "But to those who did receive Him, He granted ability to become God's children, that is, to those who believe in His name; who owe their birth neither to human blood, nor to physical urge, nor to human design, but to God" (Jn 1:12-13, Berkeley).

THE SAINT AND SERVICE

James 2:14-26

Title: Faith that Works

Text: "Can't you see that his (Abraham's) faith and his ac-

tions were, so to speak, partners—that his faith was imple-
mented by his deed?" (2:22, Phillips).

Proposition: Only true faith produces good works.

Key Word: Illustrations

Plan: In the passage before us, James illustrates a false (or
a fruitless) faith, and a true (or fruitful) faith.
  I. False faith is a fruitless faith.
     A. Illustration of a brother refusing to aid a brother or
        sister in desperate physical and material need, vv.
        14-17
     B. Illustration of demons, which believe in God, but
        continue in the service of Satan, vv. 18-20
 II. True faith is a fruitful faith.
     A. Abraham's faith expressed in works—in obeying God
        in the offering of his own son Isaac, vv. 21-24
     B. Rahab's faith expressed by her actions toward the
        people of God, vv. 25-26

Parallel Passages:

2:14—faith: 1 Co 15:1-2; Eph 2:8-10; Heb 11:7, 8, 23-30
2:17—works: Jn 6:28-29; Ro 4:4-5; Titus 2:14, 3:5-8
2:19—devils (demons) believe: Mt 8:28-29; Ac 16:17
2:21—justified: Lk 18:9-14; Ro 3:24, 28, 30; 5:1, 9; 8:33 (We
   are justified judicially by God, meritoriously by the blood,
   gratuitously by grace, conditionally by faith, evidencially
   by works.)
2:23—righteousness: Is 64:6; Ro 3:20-22, 25-26; Phil 3:8-9
2:26—dead: Eph 2:1; 1 Ti 5:6; 1 Jn 5:12

Preamble:

   In the first chapter of James, the author shows us that faith
in God should keep us joyfully triumphant throughout our
trials and tribulations in this tempestuous world. He gave
us many good reasons why we should "smile at the storm."

He told us how the Word of God was to feed our faith and to fire our enthusiasm to practice that faith.

In the second chapter, James proceeds to show us that the reality of our faith is tested by the way we treat the people whom we consider do not belong to our particular group.

In the portion before us now, at the end of chapter two, James contrasts true faith with false faith. In order to make sure that his readers get the sermon straight, he uses two illustrations of a fruitless faith and provides us with two illustrations of a fruitful faith.

Précis:

Faith means far more than just a mental assent to the truth of God's Word. The demons believe in God; they believe in the deity of Christ; they believe in hell; they are quite orthodox and very conservative in their theology; but they are loveless. They lack compassion. They are in league with Satan to destroy men, not to save them.

Saving faith also involves the mind, the emotions, and the will; or, you might say, our concepts, our character, and our conduct. Faith first brings us into vital fellowship with God through the risen Saviour. Then when the vertical relationship is a reality, it immediately affects the horizontal relationship toward mankind.

James illustrates the importance of having a faith that works. If a brother or sister in Christ is destitute and comes to a Christian for the necessities of life, the response to an evident need will expose either the vanity or the verity of that Christian's profession. Abraham's faith lay at the root of all his works. His obedience to God was the expression of his trust in God. Rahab, sinful and unworthy, heard of the wonderful redemption of God's people out of Egypt, confessed her faith, and exhibited her faith by her works. Saving faith is a faith that works.

Application:

Is your faith dead or alive? Is it only in your head or in your heart as well? Does your faith work? Are you correct in your doctrine but corrupt in your practice? Are you more concerned about your dispensational charts than you are about your dispositional quirks? Do you have compassion? Do you drive many miles to Bible conferences to escape confrontation with reality at home? Do you return bragging about the speakers, but have no testimony for the Saviour?

A correction of this hypocrisy would precipitate a revival in the church. The reason why the modern church is so ineffective in this century is that it has had too many pretenders in its pews, too many preachers and pastors who care more about pleasing men than God, too many phonies. Abraham was a friend of God. We can be His friends too when we are ready to obey Him in all that He is asking us to do.

We have polarized faith and works. Let us bring them together to the equator of spiritual sunlight. Thus the world will be convinced that the Christian faith is a faith that works.

The Saint and his Speech

James 3:1-18

Title: Taming the Tongue

Text: "The tongue is as dangerous as any fire, with vast potentialities for evil. It can poison the whole body; it can make the whole of life a blazing hell. No one can tame the human tongue" (3:6, 8, Phillips).

Proposition: The human tongue can only be controlled by God's resources.

Key Word: Reasons

Plan: Certain things can only be controlled with outside power.

I. There are many things that can be controlled by man.

    A. A huge horse, v. 3
    B. A sizable ship, v. 4
    C. Wild creatures, v. 7
 II. The tongue cannot be controlled by man, v. 8.
    A. It is small but powerful, v. 5.
    B. It is affected by hell, v. 6.
    C. It is unruly and poisonous, v. 8.
III. The tongue should be controlled.
    A. It affects the whole body, v. 2, 6.
    B. It should be used for blessing, vv. 9-12.
IV. The tongue can be controlled by wisdom from above, vv. 13-18.

Parallel Passages:

3:1—masters (Gk. *didaskaloi,* "teachers"): 1 Ti 1:7; 2 Ti 4:1-4; Titus 1:9-11
3:2—word: Ps 119:133, 172; Pr 15:26; Mt 12:36; Ja 1:26
3:5—tongue: Ps 5:9; 15:3; 39:1, 3; 50:19; 120:2-3; Pr 6:16-19; 10:20
3:10—mouth: Ps 32:8-9; Mt 10:32-33; Ro 3:14, 19; 10:9-10
3:11—fountain: Jn 4:13-14; 7:37-39; Rev 7:17, 21:6

Preamble:

When a doctor examines a patient, he usually asks to see the tongue. The tongue tells a tale in more ways than one. God gave us two ears and one tongue. This may suggest that we should do twice as much listening as we do talking.

Our scripture passage deals with the saint and his speech. James here cautions us to exercise great care in the use of our tongue. A person without proper control of his tongue is like a wild horse on the range, a rudderless ship, and a fire raging out of control. The damage done through careless speech is infinite. When people who claim to be Christians are loose with language, they are servants of Satan, not servants of God. The tongue is like a wild beast. But there is no beast in all of God's creation that is more difficult to tame than the tongue. This condition can be corrected. We cannot correct it; God can. We can cooperate by coming to Him in complete acknowledgment of our human helplessness.

Précis:

A teacher of divine truth is responsible to men and accountable to God for his doctrine. A mature man will be recognized by his use of the tongue. A huge horse, a sizeable ship, a flaming forest, and a ferocious beast can be controlled by relatively small instruments. But while men can control horses, ships, fires, or wild beasts, they cannot control their own tongues. The human inability to control the tongue requires God's resources.

Application:

Some Christians seem to be operating a hotel, taking in boarders whose pet pastime is idle chatter. These transients are here today and gone tomorrow, but all the time they are on the premises, they sow discord. Let those who traffic in such dissension be careful that this sinful business doesn't lead to spiritual bankruptcy.

Proper use of the tongue is a miracle, but God can do what men cannot do. He can put a well of living water within our hearts. From that well will issue streams of praise. The woman of Samaria found that fountain when she met Christ at Sychar many years ago. You can meet Him today.

Is your speech under supervision? Do you recognize the infinite and incalculable potential of your tongue for evil and for good? Your tongue tells what you are. A tongue full of deadly poison reveals corrupt character. If the fountain of your heart is foul, the spring needs attention. It does not help to paint the pump if there is poison water coming from the well. Reformation is not the answer; regeneration is.

God created your tongue. He wants it used for His glory. Sin has fouled up the well. Christ can supply you with His new well. He is that living water. The Holy Spirit is the provision of Christ for the thirsty. The blessed triune God provides the answer. You may come now and from this moment speak from a new heart.

THE SAINT AND SAGACITY

James 3:13-18

Title: Wise or Otherwise?

Text: "Who is a wise man . . . among you? let him shew out of a good conversation his works with meekness of wisdom" (3:13).

Proposition: We should be able to distinguish marks of true and false wisdom.

Key Word: Marks

Plan: Both true and false wisdom have distinguishing marks.

I. The marks of true wisdom, vv. 13, 17-18
   A. A good life, v. 13
   B. Meekness, v. 13
   C. Purity of life, v. 17
   D. Quiet gentleness, v. 17
   E. Compatibility, v. 17
   F. Courtesy, v. 17
   G. Affability, v. 17
   H. Absence of partiality, v. 17
   I. Absence of hypocrisy, v. 17

II. The marks of false wisdom, vv. 14-16
   A. Bitterness, v. 14
   B. Jealousy, v. 14
   C. Selfishness, v. 14
   D. A restless heart, v. 14
   E. Incompatibility, v. 14
   F. Pride and self-glory, v. 14
   G. Temporal values, v. 15
   H. Sensual lusts, v. 15
   I. Devilishness, v. 15
   J. Confusion, v. 16
   K. Every evil work, v. 16

Parallel Passages:

3:13—wisdom: 1 Ki 4:29; Ps 111:10; Pr 2:6; 1 Co 1:17-30
3:13—meekness: Ps 25:9, 147:6, 149:4; Mt 11:29, 21:5; Eph
  4:2
3:14—bitter envying: 1 Sa 18:5-11, 19:10-11; Mt 27:18; 1 Ti
  6:4; Titus 3:3; Ja 3:16; 1 Pe 2:1
3:15—sensual (Gk. *psuchikos*, "soulish" or "natural"): 1 Co
  2:14, 15:44, 15:46
3:15—devilish (demoniacal): Mt 4:24; 8:16, 28, 33
3:16—confusion (tumult): 2 Co 6:5, 12:20
3:17—peaceable: Is 32:18; Ro 12:18; Heb 12:11
3:17—gentle: 2 Sa 22:36; 2 Co 10:1, Titus 3:2; 1 Pe 2:18

Preamble:

A few people are wise; most are otherwise. What makes
the difference? James dares to set down sure signs of distinction. A man may be well educated and yet be a fool. A man
may have many university degrees but not know who he is,
what he is here for, nor where he is going. A man may rule
an empire, yet not be able to rule his own spirit.

The previous portion of James chapter three dealt with the
subject of speech. Listen a little while to the language of a
stranger, and you will soon discover whether that person
is wise or unwise. Listen not only to the talk, but to the tone.
A wise man may sometimes be identified by his silence. In
the passage before us, James uses the scissors of spiritual in-
sight to separate two vastly different types of wisdom which
govern the conduct of men, earthly wisdom and heavenly
wisdom. Each one is earmarked. The conclusion leaves no
doubt as to who is wise and who is otherwise.

Précis:

A wise man is humble, for he realizes how little he knows
in terms of all there is to know. The most knowledgeable per-

son knows only a small fraction of knowledge. A wise man is marked by meekness, purity of life, quiet gentleness, common courtesy, sociability, integrity. And all this is the result of not only natural endowment but supernatural enduement. God is the source and center of all true wisdom. He is the point of reference about which life and learning must revolve. (The book of Ecclesiastes amplifies and verifies the vanity of the pursuit of knowledge when God is ignored.)

The wisdom of this world is foolishness. A person who boasts about his wisdom, brags about his wit, bluffs his way to the front, is like a big balloon and liable to blow up at any moment. Such men are marked by their arrogance, bitterness of spirit, selfishness, dishonesty, confusion on all fronts, earthly-mindedness, and every kind of evil. This state is the state of Satan's kingdom and of all his subjects.

Application:

Are you wise or otherwise? Is your life governed by the wisdom that is from God above? Or by a kind of earthly wisdom, that rules God out of its thoughts? You are the arbiter in this matter. Let Christ, who is made unto us wisdom, be enthroned in the citadel of your mind. Let His meekness, His purity, His gentleness, His congeniality, His impartiality, His grace, and His greatness shine out through you. Be transformed. Stop keeping Christ imprisoned, locked up behind the bars of your carnality. Let the glorious Saviour shed forth the beams of His loveliness to the end of the world through your broken spirit. This is the way of wisdom.

THE SAINT AND SUPPLICATION
JAMES 4:1-12

Title: Believers at the Battlefront

Text: "From whence come wars and fightings among you?

Humble yourselves in the sight of the Lord, and he shall lift you up" (4:1, 10).

Proposition: There are two steps to personal victory in prayer.

Key Word: Steps

Plan: Each Christian must take two steps to have personal victory in prayer.

I. The first step is to see the need for personal victory.
   A. There are conflicts among the brethren, v. 1.
   B. These conflicts among brethren originate in the human heart, v. 1.
   C. Covetousness is a contradiction of Christianity, v. 2.
   D. Hatred in the heart makes prayer undesirable, v. 2.
   E. Human lusts conflict with God's desire, v. 3.
   F. People prefer to please the world more than God, v. 4.
   G. People ignore the right of the Holy Spirit to rule, v. 5.

II. We must also comply with the conditions for personal victory.
   A. Devotion to the Word of God, v. 5
   B. Readiness to yield to the tender entreaties of the Spirit of God, v. 5
   C. Willingness to humble ourselves that we might receive grace from God, vv. 6, 10
   D. Submission to God in any and all areas where there has been conflict and controversy, v. 7
   E. Positive resistance to Satan, v. 7
   F. Drawing near to God in true contrition for past failures, vv. 8-9
   G. Letting the law of love instead of a critical spirit govern our life, vv. 11-12

Parallel Passages:

4:1—lusts that war in your members: Ro 7:14-23; Gal 5:16-21

4:2—covet (desire): 1 Ki 21:1-24; Lk 12:15-21; Eph 5:5; 1 Ti 6:9-11

4:3—ask: 1 Ki 3:5-14; Mt 7:7; Lk 11:5-13; Jn 14:13-14

4:5—dwelleth: Ps 91; 1 Co 3:16, 6:19; 2 Co 6:16; Eph 3:17

4:6—more grace: Jn 1:14-17; 2 Co 9:8; 1 Ti 1:13-15

4:6—proud: Pr 8:13, 16:18; Is 16:6; 1 Ti 3:6; 1 Jn 2:16

4:7—submit to God: Gen 22:2-3, 15-18; Lk 22:42; Ro 6:13

4:7—resist the devil: Mt 4:1-11; 1 Pe 5:7-9; Rev 12:9-11

4:11—judgeth: Mt 7:1-5; Ro 14:1-15; 1 Co 11:31-32

Preamble:

Believers are at the battlefront. The fight is fierce. The foe is furious. Our adversary, Satan, has marshaled all his hosts to destroy our Advocate and His church. The gates of hell shall not prevail, but they do often prevent the saints of God from pressing on to victory. This conflict of the ages is spiritual and its front line is prayer. It is not a fight against flesh and blood. It is a battle against unseen spiritual hosts of wickedness. These hellish hosts incite men, even the children of God, to war with one another and thus to divert their attention from the real foe. All believers should be united in faith, love, and prayer to battle through to victory against the devil and all his legions.

The reason why the Christian church is not reporting more prayer victories on foreign fronts is that she has been too occupied with a civil war on the home front. James, in his fourth chapter, points out the problem and provides the answer. This passage marks out the road to revival. Whenever and wherever God's people have been willing to follow faithfully the steps indicated here, it has resulted in restoration and spiritual victory.

Précis:

The continual conflicts among professing Christians stem from carnality and covetousness. This condition chokes prayer, by which means alone the church can proceed to victory. Though active, the church cannot be effective till this condition is corrected.

The way to correct this condition is through thorough repentance. This requires our reverent attention to the Word of God and the wooings of the Spirit of God, and humbling ourselves before God until we find grace to right the wrongs among us. It also involves submission to God, resisting the devil, contrition for sin, cleansing, and taking God seriously. It means the riddance of a critical and caustic spirit, a reverential fear of God, and the saturation of our hearts with the love of God, the only law by which Christian life is to be governed. Any individual or any church that will meet these conditions can have a revival whenever they want it. And such a church would be both militant and triumphant. A church out of fellowship with God is like a bone out of joint. We cannot war against Satan while warring with the saints.

Application:

Are you on the battlefield for Christ and His kingdom? Has your attention been diverted to a war against flesh and blood, when the real foe is Satan? Change your tactics. Submit to God. Resist the devil. Get on praying ground. Do more fighting on your knees. Live in touch with your Commander, and you will be more than a conqueror.

THE SAINT AND SELF-WILL

James 4:13-17

Title: Putting God in Our Plans

Text: "Your remarks should be prefaced with, 'If it is the Lord's will, we shall still be alive and shall do so-and-so'" (Ja 4:15, Phillips).

Proposition: God must have priority in all our planning.

Key Word: Reasons

Plan: Unless God has priority in our planning, we will miss the real meaning of life.

I. We must put God in our planning because life is very uncertain.
   A. Our godless planning is an exercise in futility, v. 13.
   B. Our true values in life are not temporal, v. 14.

II. We must put God in our planning because life is very short.
   A. The eternal must be determined here and now, v. 15.
   B. The temporal must be filled with the eternal, vv. 16-17.

III. Life can be full of usefulness and fruitfulness if we put God in our planning.

Parallel Passages:

4:13—tomorrow: Pr 27:1; Mt 6:30; Lk 12:16-19; 1 Co 15:32
4:14—a little time: Job 7:6; Ps 90:3-12, 102:3; Ja 1:9-11
4:15—if the Lord will: Jn 6:38; Ac 9:6; Ro 15:3-6; Phil 2:1-5
4:16—boastings: Ps 49:6, 94:4; Is 14:12-15; Dan 4:28-34
4:17—doeth it not: Mt 25:24-30; Lk 12:47-48; Ja 2:14-17

Preamble:

What are your plans for the future? Do you have the date set, the calendar marked, the engagement fixed? Do you dream day and night of a quick climb to fame and fortune? Do you have the money made, the house furnished, the car bought, the children educated, the world tour completed, your greatness duly recognized, the world at your feet?

It is not wrong to dream. When asleep, we can scarcely avoid dreaming. But when we are awake, our dreams should be less fanciful and more factual. They should take God into account. Some people let their minds become escape mechanisms, and like the astronauts, they blast off to some distant place of fantasy. But it is important to come back to earth.

In the passage before us, James tells us very plainly that it is a sin to leave God out of our reckoning. Unless God has priority in our planning, we will miss the real meaning of life.

Précis:

All business in the life of a believer is God's business. Each one should recognize God as a rightful partner in all plans and pursuits. It is ungodly to live without God. This attitude we should adopt daily, that if this day were our last day on earth, it would be lived in the will of God and for the glory of God. To know this and not to do it, is to practice evil.

Application:

Does God have priority in your planning? Are you missing the real meaning of life? Is the Lord Jesus Christ your sovereign as well as your Saviour? Is He president as well as resident? Does He hold the key to every room in your heart, your home? In planning for tomorrow, attend to His leading today.

THE SAINT AND THE SECOND COMING OF CHRIST
James 5:1-12

Title: Harvesttime is Coming

Text: "The coming of the Lord is at hand" (Ja 5:8, A.S.V.).

Proposition: What counts in life is what is harvested in the end.

Key Word: Inducements

Plan: The inducements for a full life can be observed in the light of Christ's coming.

I. Man's shortsighted living has induced injustice.
    A. The misery of abused privilege, vv. 1-3
    B. The rewards of ungodly gains, vv. 4-6

II. God's design for the ages should induce steadfastness.
    A. Our fruit-bearing is precious, v. 7.
    B. Our steadfastness purifies our relationships, vv. 8-9.

III. God's vindication of the prophets should induce purity of life.
    A. God's vindication of the prophets is an example, vv. 10-11*a*.
    B. God's reward of Job's patience should teach us, vv. 11-12.

IV. Life is intended to have a full end and not an empty one. The harvest is coming, and "the path of the just . . . shineth more and more unto the perfect day."

Parallel Passages:

5:1—rich: Pr 11:28; Is 2:7-22; Lk 16:19-31; Rev 3:14-20
5:2—corrupted: Mt 12:33; Lk 12:33; Eph 4:22; 1 Pe 3:4
5:3—last days: Mt 24:3-25, 46; 1 Ti 4:1; 2 Ti 3:1-6; Heb 1:1-2. (Some scholars regard the expression to encompass the entire time between His advents; others apply the reference to the last days of this church age.)
5:4—Lord of sabaoth ("Lord of hosts," implying hosts of angels): Dan 7:10; Lk 2:13; 2 Th 1:7-10; Jude 14-15
5:5—pleasure: Ps 36:8; Pr 21:17; Ec 2:1; Is 58:13; Phil 2:13
5:7—patient: Lk 21:19; Ro 5:3; Col 1:11; 1 Th 1:3; Heb 12:1
5:7, 8—coming of the Lord: Mt 24:3, 27, 37, 39; 1 Co 15:23; 1 Th 3:13, 4:15, 5:23; 2 Th 2:1, 8; 2 Pe 1:16
5:12—swear: Mt 5:34; Mk 6:23; Lk 1:73; Heb 6:13

Preamble:

Christ is coming to earth again. This is the unanimous testimony of the Old Testament prophets, of New Testament

apostles, and of Christ Himself, the Prophet and Apostle par
excellence. The Scriptures declare that He will come per-
sonally, visibly, and suddenly and that he will come in great
power and in great glory. He will come with a mighty multitude of His angels to wrest this wicked world from the iron
grasp of all oppressors. Christ the King is coming to estab-
lish His kingdom. Christ the Lord is coming to overpower
all opposition. The coming of the Lord is the coming of the
day of the Lord, that crucial and most climactic day of both
history and prophecy.

The coming of the Lord is the subject of this Scripture just
read. Practical James shows how this hope should affect conduct, not effect controversy. Too often, teachers and preachers have allowed this timely topic of the approaching advent
of Christ to ignite heated discussion. Granted that we all
have our biases, let us at the same time remain teachable,
and above all, practical and scriptural in our interpretations.
There are some significant lessons to be learned from the
Word before us.

Précis:

In the last days of this church age, there will be bitter contention between the rich and the poor, between capital and
labor, accompanied by so much cruel oppression, so much
pleasure-seeking and wanton wickedness, that divine intervention will become imperative. Christ will come to right all
wrong. This is the shining star in that night of trial, when
the saints will be tested with respect to their patient endurance. Like the farmer who must wait patiently for the harvest, like the prophets who endured unto death, like Job who
lost all before he gained all, Christians must patiently wait
for His coming. They are to rejoice in their trials. They are
to know peace and not panic, in the midst of their tribulations. They are to refrain from the use of any mixed oaths in
times of tension. Their yes must mean yes, and their no must

mean no. In the final stage of this age it will be Christ or antichrist.

Application:

Are you ready for the coming of Christ? Are you living this day for that day? Are you faithful in the stewardship of that which God has committed to your trust? Are you ready to endure right to the end and consider it an honor to suffer for His sake? God's gold must be refined. It is better to go through the refining here than at that judgment day, when Christ comes with His refining fire to test every man's works.

THE SAINT AND SICKNESS

James 5:13-20

Title: Praying for the Sick

Text: "The prayer of faith shall save the sick" (5:15).

Proposition: The prayer of faith shall save the sick on three conditions.

Key Word: Conditions

Plan: The prayer of faith shall save the sick on these conditions.

I. The sick one must solicit help.
    A. By personal prayer, that is, in looking to God, v. 13
    B. By personally requesting the help of the leaders in the church, v. 14*a*

II. The leaders must be willing to look to the Lord.
    A. In united prayer ("let them pray"), v. 14
    B. In dependence on the Holy Ghost ("anointing him with oil"), v. 14
    C. For God's glory alone ("in the name of the Lord"), v. 14
    D. In faith ("the prayer of faith"), v. 15*a*

III. All concerned must be willing to right whatever wrongs
may hinder the answer.
  A. When the sick one is willing to get right if he is not
     right, v. 15
  B. When all are willing to confess and correct the sins
     that separate them from each other as members of
     His body, v. 16
  C. When prayer is directed at the healing of spiritual
     sicknesses that render the church so weak that it has
     become immobile, v. 16
  D. When all are right with God, the prayer of any indi-
     vidual is then effectual and will avail much, v. 16
  E. The power of prayer demonstrated in the life of
     Elijah, vv. 17-18
  F. A general application of the above procedure, vv.
     19-20

Parallel Passages:

5:13—afflicted: Gen 41:52; Ps 34:19; Is 48:10, 63:9; 2 Co
6:4; Ja 5:10
5:14—sick: Lk 7:10; Jn 4:46, 11:2; Ac 9:37; Phil 2:26-27
5:14—elders: Ac 14:23; 15:2, 4, 6, 22, 23; 1 Ti 5:17; Titus
1:5-9
5:14—church: Acts 13:1, 15:41, 16:5, 20:17, 28; 1 Co 1:2, 7:17
5:15—prayer of faith: Mt 8:13, 9:28-31, 21:22, 25, 32; Mk
11:23-24
5:16—confess: Ps 32:5; Pr 28:13; Dan 9:20; 1 Jn 1:9
5:17—Elijah prayed earnestly: 1 Kings 17:1; 17:17-23; 18:24,
36-39
5:19, 20—convert: Mt 18:3; Lk 22:31-32; Jn 12:37-41; Ac
28:27

Preamble:

We live in a sick society. The moans and groans of suffer-
ers over the whole wide world bear loud testimony to the

fallen state of Adam's race. Creation yearns for redemption. In spite of pills and hospitals, doctors and druggists, tonics and vitamins, millions each year die with disease. What answer do the Scriptures give to this widespread suffering? We would expect that practical James would not omit such a timely topic.

While there are many sorts of sickness plaguing people everywhere, we shall have to limit our discussion here to physical sickness. This is most likely the intent of the original writer, though there may be some allusion to spiritual sickness.

Should Christians call a doctor? Yes! But is the family physician the *first* resort in sickness? What if a doctor is not available? What about people whose condition is beyond human help? Does God use doctors? Yes! But does He work only through human agencies, or may He work entirely apart from such? What about faith healers, mind cures, healings claimed by false cults, witchdoctors, and pagan priests? Does God answer prayer? Why are so many of God's saintliest saints sick? Why are their prayers seemingly ignored? Why is God silent? How are we to believe in His benevolence and omnipotence in the light of what we know of human suffering? All of these questions may not be answered in this text. We may never know on this side of heaven. Let us nevertheless learn all we can from this passage.

Précis:

When afflicted or sick, each one should practice turning first to the great Physician, the Lord Jesus Christ. If too sick to pray, call the elders. Their united prayer in complete dependence on the Holy Spirit, as symbolized by the oil, when for the glory of God alone, will arrest the sickness and result in his recovery. Sickness is not necessarily the result of some personal sin. But if there is sin, either in the one sick, or among the elders, or in the local church, this barrier to blessing can be removed. Since God has provided full forgiveness, we ought also to forgive one another and be ready to right every wrong among us as a local assembly. When Christians are right with God and with one another, then prayer is effectual. God is sovereign in all of nature, as demonstrated through Elijah. Elijah was not a superman. He was a man who was right with God. God is looking for such men today. If a Christian brother gets off the course and strays from the truth, his recovery will avoid his having to be removed, and a multitude of sins will be avoided by him and others under his baneful influence. A revival, as in the early church, would witness wonders.

Application:

The church is an organism as well as an organization. As a member of the body of Christ, the church is intended to participate in His divine life. Physical as well as spiritual health should be enjoyed by all who are united to Him in faith. Sin, among the brethren, is the barrier that blockades blessing, and the cause of many premature deaths.

Sickness, being subnormal for those united to a living and resurrected Saviour, is a call to united prayer and to the removal of all hindrances to answered prayer. It is a call to revival.

Are you right with God? Are you ready to get right? Is someone physically sick because you are spiritually sick? Many want to see Pentecostal power but they are not willing to seek Pentecostal purity. This blindness affects our discernment. God is not real to many; to some, He is dead. What about you?

James, in this letter, invites his brethren to be triumphant in trial, practical in faith, sweet in their disposition, humble in attitude, patient under oppression, and ready to remove any barrier to revival, just as the disciples had to take away the stone before Lazarus could come forth.

PART 4

THE BOOK STUDIED

THE WORD-STUDY METHOD

The word-study method is designed to stimulate students to think. Many Christians are living on predigested spiritual food. They repeat in parrotlike fashion what someone else has written or spoken. Meditation has become a lost art.

Several of these word studies represent the work of students in my classes. This accounts for the style variations that the reader will see with each study.

Crucial words have been selected. The students were asked to answer two basic questions for each word chosen:

1. What is the meaning of the word?
2. What is the message of the word?

In seeking to probe the meaning of the word, we shall consider dictionary definitions, the Hebrew use of the word, the Greek use of the word, and, in summary, the use of the word today. Sources used in this study are included in the Bibliography.

In reaching out for the message of the word, consideration will be given to its application to the original readers and its application to us today.

TEMPTATION

peirasmois—1:2

(The Saint and the Storm—1:1-12)

MEANING

Dictionary definitions:

In Latin literature, *temptare* or *tentare* means:
1. To try the strength of, to try, to stretch

2. To try to persuade a person; induce, entice, allure, especially to do something sensually pleasurable or immoral
3. To arouse desire in; be inviting to; to attract (e.g., "That pie tempts me.")
4. To provoke or run the risk of provoking
5. To dispose or incline strongly (e.g., "I am tempted to accept.")

Hebrew lexicons:

According to Gesenius, the Hebrew verb *nasah* comes from an Arabic root, meaning "to smell, to try." He goes on to say that the primary idea differs from the Hebrew word *bachan*, which means "to try by the touch," as if to prove by a touchstone.

In the Piel (a form of the Hebrew verb), the infinitive *nisah* means, "to try, to prove anyone."

1. In 1 Kings 10:1, the queen of Sheba came to prove Solomon with hard questions, that is, to examine the wisdom of Solomon. (See also 2 Ch 9:1; Dan 1:12, 14.)
2. God is said to try or prove men by adversity, in order to prove their faith (Gen 22:1; Ex 16:4; Deu 8:2, 16, 13:4; Judg 2:22).
3. Men are said to prove or tempt God when they doubt His power and aid (Ex 17:2; Deu 6:16; Ps 78:18, 41, 56; Is 7:12).
4. It is also used in the sense of "to try, to attempt, to make a trial, to venture" (Deu 4:34, 28:56; 1 Sa 17:39; Judg 6:39; Job 4:2).

Greek lexicons:

The Greek word *peirasmos* is used in three ways:

1. Test, trial
2. Temptation, enticement to sin
   a) From Satan (Lk 4:13)

b) From without or from within a person (1 Ti 6:9; Rev 3:10)

3. Testing of God by men (Num 14:22; Deu 6:16, 9:22; Heb 3:8-9)

One of its cognates, *peira*, used in Hebrews 11:3, refers to an intensive trial of one's faith under strong duress.

Another relative, the verb *peirazo*, means:

1. Try, attempt (Ac 9:26, 16:7, 24:6)
2. Try, make trial of, put to the test, to discover what kind of a person someone is
   a) Used in a good sense of God or Christ, who put men to the test so they may prove themselves true (1 Co 10:13; Heb 11:17; Gen 22:1; Ex 22:20; Old Testament references taken from the Septuagint)
   b) Used in a bad sense, in order to bring out something to be used against the person who is being tried; Jesus was so treated by his opponents (Mt 16:1; 19:3; 22:18)
   c) Used in a bad sense also of enticement to sin (Gal 6:1; Ja 1:13)
   d) Used also to speak of a trial of God by men; men put God to the test to discover whether He really can do a certain thing, whether He notices sin and is able to punish it (Ex 17:2; Num 14:22; Is 7:12; 1 Co 10:9)

It is used in Numbers 14:22 in a bad sense to show that men tempt God, provoking Him to wrath by deliberate insolence, doing this repeatedly until God has to visit judgment upon them. Their daring disobedience lasted forty years (Heb 3:9).

In Matthew 4:1, there is a dual activity involved. The Holy Spirit led Christ into the wilderness to demonstrate to all mankind that Christ could confront the great archenemy of our souls and emerge the victor in the fray.

At the same time, Satan sought to gain empire over the Son of man as Son of God, but was foiled. Christ had divested Himself of His divine rights, not of His essential deity. Thus He became the target of a terrible attack but withstood Satan in this great conflict of the ages. As man, Christ was tested in all points as a man. Endued with the Spirit (as we humans can be and need to be) in order to withstand the onslaught of Satan's assaults, Christ is both our example and our deliverer. He trusted God (Heb 2:13). So must we.

Summary:

We have traced the use of "temptation" and its cognates throughout the Scriptures. The meaning of the word must in each case be determined by its use in the context.

The basic idea of the word is "trial." God may be trying men, or men may be trying God. Men may be tried from without, from within, by men, by God, by Satan. Men may be tried in a good sense or in an evil sense, to reveal strength or weakness. Satan tempted Christ to see if He would sin; the Holy Spirit led Christ into the wilderness to demonstrate that He would not sin.

MESSAGE

To the first readers:

James wanted his Jewish Christian brethren, scattered among the nations as seed scattered in a field, to realize a law of the harvest, that there can be no reaping unless there is first a time of seeding. They are to rejoice with unmitigated joy.

To modern readers:

Trials, though coming to us in many hues, afford us an opportunity to develop sound and steadfast character. Trials teach us to trust even where we cannot trace.

Trials are to be kept outside. While the storm rages on

the outside, peace is to reign within. "Let not your hearts be troubled," Jesus admonished His disciples. An outside temptation looks to find a traitor on the inside with whom to conspire. If we let the trial drive a wedge between us and God, and then blame God for our misery, lust uses the occasion to turn the trial into a temptation to evil. When these two join in wedlock, sin is conceived in the heart; and soon the evil union gives birth to sin; and sin separates a soul from God. If, instead of blessing God for the trials of life, we start blaming God, we fail. If a Christian lets the storm disturb his spiritual equilibrium, he becomes, like the wicked, a vessel on a storm-tossed sea. The rip-currents of trouble and tribulation bring shipwreck. The prophet Isaiah affirmed so rightly, "There is no peace, saith my God, to the wicked" (Is 57:20-21).

The trials, or temptations, referred to in this chapter, are God's employees, sent to help us discover our true condition. Under strong duress we find out whether we have any temper in the steel of our spiritual springs; or if we have enough temper to take the jolts, the bumps, the potholes, which must be encountered on the rough road. When we accept trials as part of our inheritance, through faith we may prevail. Difficulties are the very diet of those delivered out of the devil's dominion and brought under Christ's domain. Faith in God means full reliance on His wisdom, power, love, grace, and immutability. Such faith produces patience, promotes prayer, and prepares us as candidates for the crown of life on the day of Christ, the day toward which all history moves, the most crucial day of both time and eternity.

Anyone who regards such trials as temptations to evil and starts blaming God instead of blessing Him, is headed for trouble. We err grievously when we start on such a course. If pursued, that course can lead only to separation from God.

When welcomed, trials lead to an abundant life. The

Christian is a candidate for the crown of life. But when we refuse, rebel, reject, we lose our reward.

PERFECT

teleios—1:4

(The Saint and the Storm—1:1-12)

MEANING

Dictionary definitions:

1. Expert, proficient
2. Flawless, accurate, pure
3. Total, absolute, unequivocal, and whole

Hebrew lexicons:

1. *gemar*—complete, Ezra 7:12
2. *kuwn*—to be prepared, Pr 4:18
3. *kaliyl*—complete, Eze 16:14
4. *shalem*—full, whole (used fifteen times), 1 Ki 8:61
5. *tam*—plain, undefiled, perfect (used ten times), Job 1:1
6. *tamiym*—unblemished, complete (used eighteen times), Gen 6:9

Greek lexicons:

Uses of *perfect:*

1. *Akribōs*—accurately, diligently (used six times) Lk 1:3
2. *Artios*—fitted, perfect—2 Ti 3:17
3. *Plēroō*—to fill, make full—Rev 3:2
4. *Teleios*—ended, complete—Ja 1:4, 17, 25, 3:2

Uses of *to be perfect:*

1. *Katartizō*—to fit thoroughly, adjust (used seven times) Heb 13:21
2. *Teleioō*—to end, complete (used fifteen times) Ja 2:22

Teleios, as an adjective, signifies having reached its end, finished, complete, perfect. It is used (1) of persons (*a*) primarily of physical development, then with ethical import, fully grown, mature (1 Co 2:6, 14:20; Eph 4:13) and (*b*) to mean "complete," conveying the idea of goodness without necessary reference to maturity or what is expressed under (*a*) (Mt 5:48, 19:21; Ja 1:4, 3:2); and (2) of things, to mean "complete, perfect (Ro 12:2; 1 Co 13:10), referring to the complete revelation of God's will and ways, whether in the completed Scriptures or in the hereafter (e.g., Ja 1:4, of the work of patience).

MESSAGE

To the first readers:

The perfection of our graces is not discovered till we are subjected to varied trials. The exercise of grace must not be interrupted till it be full and perfect, till it comes to a perfect work. The Christian must aim at and press on to perfection.

To modern readers:

It is interesting to note that James starts his letter off with faith, since we usually think of works when mentioning the book of James. From this faith comes patience (v. 3) and the result of patience is our key word, *perfect*. This perfection cannot be obtained unless the Christian steps out in faith. Through this faith in Christ, our lives will be made complete, lacking nothing.

WAVERING

diakrinomenos—1:6

(The Saint and the Storm—1:1-12)

MEANING

Dictionary definitions:

1. Waver—oscillate, flicker, quiver; become unsteady, begin to give way; be irresolute or undecided between different courses or opinions, be shaken in resolution or belief
2. Doubt—feel uncertain; be undecided about, hesitate to believe or trust, call in question

Greek lexicons:

1. In the active voice—to discern, distinguish, make a distinction, separate, discriminate
2. In the middle voice—to be at variance with one's self, to hesitate, to doubt

The original word suggests not so much weakness of a faith as lack of it. The word is translated in various contexts (many of which are in the active voice) as "discern, doubt, contend, put difference, stagger, make differ, make difference, judge, be partial, wavering."

In its immediate context, it is used as contrast to true faith, which is firm, steadfast, grounded. Wavering is not entirely disbelieving, yet it is not entirely believing.

Summary:

The word was used to express what faith should not be, and to show that God will not answer doubting prayer. Wavering, doubting, hesitating all imply an unsteady hand or heart into which God does not think it wise to deposit His gifts (either "wisdom" or "any thing"). The doubter is like the surge of the sea, fluctuating between cheerful confidence and dark suspicion.

MESSAGE

To the first readers:

He that comes to God must believe that He is; not only that He exists, but that He is what the term God implied—just, loving, faithful, and so on. Believing this, the Christian will receive wisdom as well as anything else which he believes God desires to give to His children.

To modern readers:

This word is even more applicable today, because our empirical and scientifically oriented society has created an intellectual environment in which steadfast faith is becoming increasingly more difficult and, consequently, doubting and wavering are widespread, even among Christians. Humanism and monism (the view that the mind and body are inseparably united) have at best allowed one who has been strongly influenced by them to "pray to God—if there be a God—to save his soul, if he have a soul."

SOUL

psuchas—1:21

(The Saint and the Scriptures—1:18-27)

MEANING

Dictionary definition:

1. The immaterial part of man
2. The moral or emotional part of man
3. The intellectual part of man; vital principle and mental powers of animals, including man

Greek lexicons:

1. Breath, as the breath of life; the vital breath or force which animates the body and will show itself in breathing; life (of animals, Rev 8:9, 16:3; elsewhere only of man); that in which there is life; a living being; a living soul
2. The soul, as the seat of the feelings, desires, affections, aversions, will; that is, our soul, heart; one's self; the powers of one's being; differs from the body and the spirit (1 Th 5:23, "I pray God your whole spirit and soul and body be preserved blameless unto the coming of our Lord Jesus Christ.") Note: Cremer's *Lexicon* points out that the soul and body may be separated; the soul and spirit may only be distinguished.

Septuagint:

Genesis 2:7, "And the Lord God formed man of the dust of

the ground, and breathed into his nostrils the breath of life; and man became a living soul (Hebrew *nephesh* is equal to Greek *psuche*)."

Summary:

The soul is the natural life in the body; the immaterial, invisible part of man; the seat of personality; the sentient, perceptive element in man, that by which he reflects, feels, desires; also the seat of his will and his purpose and his appetites. It pertains to persons as individuals, to animate creatures, and to the inward man—the seat of the new life.

The soul carries the personality of the man. It contains the conflict between the spirit (*pneuma*) drawing it upward and the flesh (*sarx*) drawing it downward. It is saved or lost (i.e., passes into life or death) according to the choice made between the spirit and the flesh.

It is the root for such words as psychology—the science of the nature, functions and phenomena of the human soul or mind; psychoanalysis—analysis of the mind in terms of conscious and unconscious, and investigation of the interaction between the two; psychiatrist, one who treats mental disease; and psychosis, severe mental derangement involving the whole personality.

The traditional concept of the soul as a thinking substance, an entity which is as much a thing in its own right as the human body is, but which differs from the body in being immaterial and nonspatial, and which is more or less loosely connected with bodily substance to form the complete human being, has been almost totally abandoned by modern psychology and largely abandoned by recent philosophy. The human being is now considered as a single substance which has physical, biological, and psychological dimensions.

If we take *soul* to mean the personality, or that which unites a series of conscious states, we can still talk psychologically of the salvation and immortality of the soul. Even here we must believe in the power of God to keep one's personality existing after death, especially in the light of the evidence indicating that when the body dies, all life ceases.

MESSAGE

To the first readers:

The soul in James 1:21 refers to human life. Keeping in mind Matthew 22:37, "Thou shalt love the Lord thy God with all thy heart, and with all thy soul, and with all thy mind," the word seems to emphasize the will, since the emotions and intellect are expressed by "heart" and "mind." From other uses, it would include the emotions, desires (or affections), and intellect.

In the broadest sense, a person's soul is his real self, his total personality. When James refers to the salvation of one's soul, he is talking about the salvation of one's total life. The salvation of the soul is a continuous process, beginning at conversion and culminating in the judgment day. Sin must be constantly cleansed from our lives, if we are to resist being drawn aside by the "flesh" or lower nature. The word, implanted at conversion, is able to draw the soul to life in the Spirit. However, it must be received in meekness, in a humble, obedient spirit. Another prerequisite for effective salvation of the soul is the "putting away of all filthiness and overflowing of wickedness."

To modern readers:

If we define "mind" as "the seat of consciousness, thought, volition, and feeling," the saving power of the Word on the soul is actually on the person's mind. And if we note that the Greek word translated "save" in this verse is sometimes translated "heal," we see a fresh immediate result of the Word of God—the healing or renewing of a person's mind. Then, not only is "putting away all filthiness and overflowing of wickedness" a prerequisite to the working of God's Word in one's life, but also it is a result. At conversion, only the conscious part of the mind is cleansed. The subconscious, from which flow previously repressed "filthiness and wickedness" can be cleansed either when these impure thoughts, motives, and desires become conscious and thus capable of being confessed and cleansed, or when the Word of God and the mind of Christ become so much a part of one's conscious mind that the subconscious is affected.

As long as we are on earth, our souls will need the healing and saving power of the living Word of God, Jesus, who comes to us through the written Word of God, the Bible.

LIBERTY

eleutherias—1:25

(The Saint and the Scriptures—1:18-27)

MEANING

Webster's Dictionary:

1. Exemption from slavery, bondage, imprisonment, or control of another
2. Freedom from external restraint or compulsion
3. Privilege; franchise; right or immunity by grant
4. Exemption from subjection to the will of another claiming ownership or services
5. Freedom from despotic or arbitrary control
6. The power of choice; freedom from necessity; freedom from compulsion or constraint in the act of willing something

Etymology:

The word *liberty* is derived from the Old French *liberte*, from the Latin *libertas*, from *liber* meaning "free."

Scripture:

The cognates of the word *liberty* are used widely throughout Scripture:

1. In the sense of freedom, *derowr* (Lev 25:10; Is 61:1; Jer 34:8, 15, 17; Ezekiel 46:17;
2. In the sense of free, *chophshiy* (Jer 34:16)
3. In the sense of sending away or a remission, *aphesis* (Lk 4:18)
4. In the sense of a sending back or a letting loose, *anesis* (Ac 24:23)
5. In the sense of authority or privilege, *exousia* (1 Co 8:9)
6. In the sense of free or at liberty, *eleutheros* (Mt 17:26; Jn 8:33, 36; Ro 6:20, 7:3; 1 Co 7:21, 22, 9:1, 19, 12:13; Gal 3:28, 4:26, 31; Eph 6:8; Col 3:11; 1 Pe 2:16; Rev 13:16; 19:18)
7. In the sense of permitting, *epitrepō* (Ac 27:3)
8. In the sense of to set at liberty or to loose away, *apolouō* (Ac 26:32; Heb 13:23)
9. In the sense of to make free, *eleutheroō* (Jn 8:32, 36; Ro 6:18, 22; Gal 5:1)

Greek lexicons:

In the Greek New Testament, the word translated "liberty" in James 1:25 is *eleutheria*. This word is used eleven times in the New Testament and in each case is translated as "liberty":

1. Liberty to do or to omit things having no relation to salvation (1 Co 10:29); from the yoke of the Mosaic law (Gal 2:4; 5:1, 13—twice; 1 Pe 2:16); from Jewish error so blinding the mental vision that the mind does not discern the majesty of Christ (2 Co 3:17); freedom from the dominion of corrupt desires, so that we do by the free impulse of the soul what the will of God requires, *nomon teleion ton tēs eleutherias* (i.e., the Christian religion, which furnishes that rule of right living by which the liberty just mentioned is attained; Ja 1:25, 2:12); freedom from the restraints and miseries of earthly frailty

manifested in the glorious condition of the future life (Ro 8:21)

2. Fancied liberty (i.e., license, the liberty to do as one pleases; 2 Pe 2:19)

Other Sources:

Robertson's *Word Pictures in the New Testament* says, "The law of liberty—'That of liberty,' (*ton tēs eleutherias*)—explaining why it is 'perfect' (2:12, also), rests on the work of Christ, whose truth sets us free (Jno. 8:32; II Cor. 3:16; Rom. 8:2)."

The Cambridge Greek Testament had this to say: "The freedom of the law of Christ is contrasted with the bondage to minute precepts which characterized the developed Mosaic system, . . . Gal. 5:1; John 8:32; Rom. 8:15. . . . The law of Christ then is called a perfect law because it is final and complete, as distinct from the Mosaic law, which was transitory and imperfect; it is called a law of liberty because it is the expression of a Father's love for his children, not for a Master's law for slaves."

Wordsworth's Greek Testament had this encouraging comment on *nomon teleion ton tēs eleutherias*—the perfect law of liberty: "Christ has redeemed us by His blood from the slavery of sin and Satan into the glorious liberty of the Sons of God. . . . He has redeemed us from the curse of the law (Gal. 3:13), and purchased us to Himself (I Cor. 6:20; 7:23), and has thus made us free (Jn. 8:36), and has conveyed to us these blessings effected by the operation of the Holy Ghost, which is therefore called God's free Spirit (Ps. 51:12; II Cor. 3:17); and has revealed to us these things in the preaching of the Gospel, which is the perfect Law of Liberty, the Law of emancipation from evil, and of obedience to God, whose service is perfect freedom, and has bound us to obey the Law of love, and to serve one another thereby (Gal. 5:13) as servants of God (I Pet. 2:16). So that while we are free by faith, we must all serve by love. And let him take heed to obey this law of liberty, for by it he will be judged (James 2:12)."

The Cambridge Bible notes, "At the Council at which St. James presided, the law of Moses, as such, was described as a 'yoke of bondage' (Acts 15:10), even as Paul spoke of it (Gal. 5:1), and that our Lord had spoken of the Truth as that by which alone men could be made 'free indeed' (Jn. 8:32). It follows from this, almost necessarily, that James speaks of the new Law, the spiritual code of ethics, which had been proclaimed by Christ, and of which the Sermon on the Mount remains as the greatest pattern and example. That Law was characterized as giving to the soul freedom from the vices that enslave it. To look into that Law and to continue in it was to share the beatitudes with which it opened."

The Interpreter's Bible adds further to our understanding of liberty, by commenting, "Are law and liberty at odds? Many assume them to be so. Law restricts and restrains; liberty unlocks all doors. To be able to do exactly as one pleases, to have no master save one's mood, that is to be free. But Thomas Huxley long ago pointed out that man's worst difficulties begin when he is able to do as he pleases, for then he must decide what he pleases to do. Freedom is simply an opportunity for choice; it gives no guidance as to what the choice should be."

Summary:

The law of God is not the negation of freedom; it is the law of liberty. It is not a limitation upon vital living; it marks the direction in which life must flow, if our potentiality is to be fulfilled.

MESSAGE

To the first readers:

The man who looks into the perfect law, the law of liberty,

is the one who has discovered that the highest happiness can be attained only if he freely chooses to live in accordance with the purpose of his Creator. Restlessness, dissatisfaction, frustration, and despair are not the lot of the servant of God, but of the rebel against God.

To modern readers:

"I delight to do thy will, O my God," is not the exclamation of a slave, but of one who has discovered that in His service is perfect freedom; for only if we willingly conform to the God-given law of our being, can we be true to our essential nature as children of God. The free man knows with Augustine that there is no heart's rest outside the will of God.

Even as these last commentators have emphasized, the liberty with which Christ has set us free from the power of sin and Satan needs to be preached. Do we know that Christ has purchased pardon and freedom from all condemnation at Calvary? To say that Christians must advance a long way along the road of spirituality before they can know spiritual release from the slavery of sin is shortchanging converts to Christ. When the wonder of redemption is realized, the soul is made to shout exultingly its eternal praises to God.

RELIGION

threskeia—1:27

(The Saint and the Scriptures—1:18-27)

MEANING

Dictionary definitions:

1. Belief in a divine or superhuman power(s) to be obeyed and worshiped as the creator(s) and ruler(s) of the universe
2. Expression of this belief in conduct or ritual
3. Any specific system of belief, worship, conduct, often in-

volving a code of ethics and a philosophy, as the Christian religion, the Buddhist religion, etc.; or loosely, any system of beliefs, practices, ethical values, resembling, suggestive of, or likened to such a system
4. A state of mind or way of life expressing love for and trust in God and one's will and effort to act accordingly to the will of God
5. Any object of conscientious regard and pursuit (e.g., "Cleanliness was a religion to him.")
6. The practice of religious observance and rites

Etymology:

The English word *religion* may be derived from a first conjugation of the Latin verb, *religo*. The infinitive *religare* means "to bind back." Or, it may be derived from a third conjugation, *religo*. Its infinitive is *religere* and means "to go over again." These meanings may suggest that religion is that which binds man to his God or gods as a servant is bound to his master, or that religion is that which governs a man's daily actions or habits.

Hebrew lexicons:

The word *religion* is not used in the Old Testament.

Greek lexicons:

The Greek word *thrēskeia* is used only three times in the New Testament (Ac 26:5; Ja 1:26, 27). A cognate, an adjective, does not appear anywhere in secular Greek literature.

The word comes from a verb, *threō*, meaning "to tremble," and refers to the fear of the ancient gods. This dread led to the performance of religious rites. The noun is the ceremonial service that springs, not from love, but from fear.

James uses an adjective, *katharos*, meaning "pure," along with this word for "religion." This suggests that religion may be pure or impure.

MESSAGE

To the first readers:

The message of James to his Christian brethren was a plea to be genuine in their religion. If a man thinks (*dokei*) that he is religious, but cannot control his tongue, his religion is not genuine. Out of the abundance of the heart, the mouth speaks. True religion, pure and proceeding from God, causes conduct and conversation to issue from a heart that has been cleansed in the precious blood of Christ. That initial cleansing was to be followed by daily cleansing in the Word.

According to the context, James exposes the hypocrisy of one who hears but does not heed the Word of God. A man with a violent temper is filthy no matter how religious he *thinks* he is. Sin in a saint, especially in his speech, is reprehensible. Whenever a saint makes the discovery of such sin in his life, with meekness and contrition, he ought to be willing to confess and forsake it.

To modern readers:

One of the reasons why Christian profession has been made so unpalatable to the world is that too many Christians are hypocritical. Christians need to have their tongues bridled under the lordship of the Lord. Pure religion (Ja 1:27), pure hearts (Ac 15:9), pure minds (2 Pe 3:1), and pure souls (1 Pe 1:22) are a part of the New Testament vocabulary. We must not forget that we have been purged from our old sins.

Pure religion links man to a holy God. In such a fellowship, impurity is repulsive. Some folk have changed the label, calling sin "perverted taste"; adultery, "wife-swapping"; a drunkard, "an alcoholic"; stealing from the company, "the five-finger discount"; a prostitute, "streetwalker." Sin is not an upward stumble in man's progress. To speak of sin as "goodness in the making" is as senseless as saying that garbage is chocolate cake in the making. Get the right label on sin. Don't be drugged to death by Satan's sleeping pills. Men need to know that hell is not a mere misfortune, and sin is neither fun nor funny. An eternal hell is the destiny of the unclean, irreligious souls who spurn the only Saviour from sin, our Lord Jesus Christ. If it required so great a sacrifice as the giving of God's Son to atone for sin, then who can estimate the guilt of every sinner who rejects that free salvation?

RESPECT OF PERSONS
prosōpolēmpsiais—2:1, 9
(The Saint and Snobbery—2:1-13)

MEANING

Dictionary definitions:

The dictionary defines a "respecter of persons" as one whose behavior toward people is influenced by their social status, prestige, and so forth.

Hebrew lexicons:

The Hebrew word *masso'*, used in 2 Chronicles 19:7 along with *paniym*, suggests as a meaning "respect of faces." Very similar is the Hebrew root *nassa'*, and similar in meaning. Gesenius says concerning this word, along with the noun *paniym*, that they mean "to accept the person of anyone, a phrase properly applicable to a king or judge who receives those who come to salute him and who bring gifts, and favors their cause (see Job 13:10)."

Hence it is used:

1. In a good sense, to receive anyone's prayer, to be favorable to it, to have respect to him as a petitioner (Gen 19:21, 32:21; Job 42:8; Pr 6:35; Lam 4:16; Mal 1:8-9).
2. In a bad sense, to be partial, spoken of a judge (Lev

19:15; Deu 10:17; Job 13:8, 10; 32:21; 34:19; Ps 82:2; Pr 18:5).

Greek lexicons:

"Respect of persons" is one word in the Greek, *prosō-polēmpsiais*. This word is a compound made up of the noun *prosōpon*, which means "face, visage, countenance, the front of anything," and the noun, *lēmpsia* derived from the verb *lambanō* which means "to receive" in its primary sense, but which also means, "to apprehend by the senses, to understand, to comprehend, to seize with the mind." A very similar word, *prosōpolēmpsia*, is used in Romans 2:11, Ephesians 6:9, and Colossians 3:25. Another cognate, *aprosōpolēptōs*, is translated, "without respect of persons" (1 Pe 1:17). The verb form, found only in James 2:9, *prosōpolēpteō*, means literally, "to accept faces."

Summary:

The meaning of the word conveys this sense: it is the fault of one, who, when called on to requite or to give judgment, has respect to the outward circumstances of the person, and not his intrinsic merits, and so prefers as more worthy one who is rich, highborn, or powerful, to one who is destitute. Jude speaks of it as "having men's persons in admiration because of advantage" (v. 16). In the context of James 2:1-13, this is the meaning; and James calls this digression "sin'" (2:9), and a transgression of the law of love.

MESSAGE

To the first readers:

Snobbery is sin. It is the sin of poor people in particular. They hope to gain some personal advantage by playing up to the rich. They are willing to snub even a poor brother in Christ and kowtow to the well-dressed stranger, if only by such preferential treatment they can advance their own prestige. The text implies that this rich man seldom attended the Christian assembly. But when he did come, he came in such a dazzling array of finery that he immediately drew the attention of the whole congregation. Though in this case, it is the error of the usher, the reproof is addressed to the whole assembly, obviously an assembly of people of meager means.

To modern readers:

In the Oriental setting of this chapter, it is quite common for most of the congregation to stand. They do, however, have a few seats reserved for any nobility who might attend. In today's world, snobbery in our churches is more often the sin of the rich. We need another Amos to fearlessly proclaim God's displeasure at our neglect of the downtrodden. When we get to chapter five of James, we shall see that the great disparity between rich and poor, in the days immediately preceding Christ's return, is going to result in a great outbreak of violence. We do not justify violence; neither do we justify greed, fraud, and injustice.

James shows us in this passage that snobbery is a violation of the law of love, the royal law, under which all of God's children should live. This is a perfect law of liberty for those walking in the Spirit. It is not a sin to be rich; it is not a virtue to be poor.

The passage is not intended to teach that all men are equal. We are to respect governmental authority, not for personal advantage, but because it is the will of God (1 Pe 2:13-17). We are to honor those who are set over us in the pastoral care of the church (1 Ti 5:17).

Many poor people would like to be rich. Why? The motive needs careful examination. If some people who were poor yesterday were made rich today, they would be poor again tomorrow. Why? In a word: character. And who can create correct character? God. And He is available through Christ, the Saviour, the mediator, the only one capable to bridge that great gap between God and man. And it was He who warned all of us in Luke 12:15, "Take heed, and beware of covetousness: for a man's life consisteth not in the abundance of the things which he possesseth."

Favoritism has divided homes, churches, communities, countries. There are not only generation gaps but gaps between brothers and sisters, mothers and fathers—members of the same generation. There are barriers between the rich and the poor, the educated and the less educated, the blacks and the whites. Churches are too fragmented to care for one another. These problems stem from favoritism that engenders snobbery and contempt. God's love is both universal and individual. His love is the divine provision for human destitution.

BLASPHEMY

blasphēmousin—2:7

(The Saint and Snobbery—2:1-13)

MEANING

Dictionary definition:

Webster says that "blaspheme" comes from the Greek *blasphēmeō* meaning "to speak evil of." It means "to speak irreverently or profanely of or to God or about sacred things." It means "to curse or revile."

Greek lexicons:

Blasphēmousin comes from the verb *blasphēmeō* meaning, "to speak abusively, to rail, to calumniate, to speak evil of often with men or things" (used specifically of God: Rev 16:11; the Holy Spirit: Lk 12:10; the divine name or doctrines: 1 Ti 6:1).

An Expository Dictionary of New Testament Words:

W. E. Vine says that to blaspheme is "to rail at or revile, is used (*a*) in a general way, of any contumelious speech, reviling, calumniating, railing at etc., as of those who railed at Christ, e.g. Matt. 27:39; Mark 15:29; Luke 22:65 (R.V. "reviling"); 23:39; (*b*) of those who speak contemptuously of God or of sacred things, e.g., Matt. 9:3; Mark 3:28; Ro 2:24; I Ti 1:20; 6:1; Rev 13:6; 16:9, 11, 21."

Summary:

Blasphēmeō is practically confined to speech defamatory of the divine majesty. There is no noun in the original representing the English "blasphemer." This is expressed either by the verb, or by the adjective, *blasphēmos.* Whenever the Bible uses the word *blasphemy,* it pertains to some person of the Trinity.

According to Christ's teaching concerning blasphemy against the Holy Spirit (e.g., Mt 12:32), anyone who has the evidence of the Lord's power before his eyes and declares it to be satanic, exhibits a condition of heart beyond divine illumination and therefore hopeless. Divine forgiveness would be inconsistent with the moral nature of God. As to the Son of man, in His state of humiliation, there might be misunderstanding, but not so when the Holy Spirit's power is demonstrated.

MESSAGE

To the first readers:

James speaks against the rich who blaspheme the name of Christ by their actions in oppressing the poor by taking them to court. In so doing they speak contemptuously of Him and His religion.

James is also speaking to the Christian brethren, because by their actions they are blaspheming Christ and not living the Christian life. They favor the rich for personal gain. James is saying that God has chosen the poor to be rich in faith.

To modern readers:

It is easy for a man of wealth to depend more on his riches than on the Lord. Many who profess the name of Christ, despise the poor. James is showing that love and kindness should be shown equally to all by those who have real faith in the Lord Jesus Christ. Christians may blaspheme the name of Christ, not only by words, but by their actions.

LOVE

agapēseis—2:8

(The Saint and Snobbery—2:1-13)

MEANING

Dictionary definitions:

Love means to have a feeling of strong personal attachment induced by sympathetic understanding, or of ties of kinship; ardent affection; affectionate devotion; paternal benevolence; strong liking; fondness, goodwill; tender and passionate affection for one of the opposite sex.

New Testament:

Agapaō is used 142 times, and its verbal form is translated "love" 135 times, and its adjectival form, "beloved," seven times. *Agapēseis* is the second singular, future indicative active tense of the verb *agapaō*. The noun *agapē* (love), is used 114 times in the New Testament. The adjective *agapētos* (beloved, dear) is used sixty-two times.

Greek lexicons:

The word translated "love" in the New Testament can mean the following:

1. To love, be full of goodwill and exhibit the same; feel or manifest generous concern for
2. To have a preference for, wish to, regard the welfare of
3. To take pleasure in, to delight in
4. Regarding a master, God or Christ: affectionate reverence, prompt obedience, grateful recognition of benefits received
5. To welcome with desire; long for; be faithful to
6. Denotes the love of the reason; esteem; to regard with favor on principle
    Note: *Phileō* is the love of the feelings (i.e., warm instinctive affection). It is a demonstration of *agapaō*. Hence *phileō* is never used of man's love to God; only *agapaō*. Both words are used of God's love to man.
7. A spontaneous love, irrespective of rights

An Expository Dictionary of New Testament Words:

1. *Love* is used to describe the attitude of God toward His Son, the human race, and to such as believe on the Lord Jesus Christ; to convey His will to His children concerning their attitude one toward another and toward all men; to express the essential nature of God ("God is love," 1 Jn 4:16).
2. Love can be known only from the actions it prompts.
3. It is not an impulse from the feeling; it does not always run with the natural inclinations, nor does it spend itself only upon those for whom some affinity is discovered.
4. In respect to God, *love* expresses the deep and constant love and interest of a perfect being toward entirely unworthy objects, producing and fostering reverential love in them toward the giver, a practical love toward those who are partakers of the same, and a desire to help others to seek the giver.

Summary:

Love to God and man is fundamental to Christianity and therefore to life. It is the greatest biblical commandment, and on it hang all the law and the prophets. Paul, in 1 Corinthians 13, describes it as the greatest gift of life—greater than speaking with tongues, or the gift of prophecy, or the possession of knowledge, or faith, or sacrifice. It is patient, kind, without envy, not proud; it seeks not its own, is not easily provoked; thinks no evil; doesn't rejoice in iniquity; rejoices in the truth; is forbearing, trustful, and hopeful; endures all things; and never fails.

Love, whether used of God or man, is an earnest and anxious desire for, and an active and beneficent interest in the well-being of the one loved. *Agapē* is the highest, the most perfect kind of love, implying a clear determination of will and judgment, and belonging particularly to the sphere of divine revelation.

MESSAGE

To the first readers:

James is showing that this principle underlies the teaching of impartiality. Love for one's neighbor is inconsistent with snobbery. If you love your neighbour as yourself, respect of persons will not be a problem. Furthermore, James may be implying that you could do even better if you followed Jesus' commandment to "love one another, as I have loved you" (Jn 13:34).

To modern readers:

According to Jesus, love for our neighbor is the second greatest commandment, second only to love for God. Love is both for and from God.

Who is my neighbor? To view our neighbor as anyone and everyone in this world at the present time, involves the danger of just having a vague feeling of goodwill to the masses.

Such a "love" is little better than none, since it finds no outward expression, and consequently cannot help anybody. Our neighbor is "anyone to whom we have it within our power to become helpful, even though he may be a stranger and a Samaritan" (*Pulpit Commentary*). To be practical, my neighbor is the person(s) whom I am with at present. My concern should be concentrated on those persons for the length of time I am with them, then shifted (in thoughts, feeling, and actions) to my next encounter. Love therefore cannot realistically be extended to everyone, though it should be extended to anyone encountered directly or indirectly (by mail, phone, etc.), which potentially is everyone.

What does it mean to love my neighbor as myself? Well, how do I love myself? I don't always feel fond of myself or find me attractive. Though I may think I am a nice guy sometimes, this is not self-love; rather it is a result of self-love. Furthermore, there are times when I think I am quite rotten. I get disgusted with some of the things I do and even punish myself accordingly. But my love for myself is why I am sorry to find myself doing such things. I wish I were not bad, and hope that I may be cured; that is, I wish myself good.

To love my neighbor, then, doesn't necessitate finding him attractive or thinking him to be a good person; nor does it exclude punishing him. What it means is wishing him good, wishing he were not bad, and hoping that he may be cured. It means desiring the best for him and doing that which is in my power to bring this about.

FAITH

pistin—2:14

(The Saint and Service—2:14-26)

MEANING

Dictionary definitions:

1. Acts or state of acknowledging unquestioningly the exis-

tence, power, and so on, of a supreme being and the
reality of a divine order; belief in God, revelation or the
like (e.g., an act of faith); conviction of divinity or of
divine origin, power, efficacy (now commonly used with
in; as, to have faith *in* prayer)
2. An acknowledged bond of fidelity to one's promises, or
   allegiance to duty, or to a person; loyalty
3. Assurance, authority; credit; as, the faith of the foregoing
   narrative
4. That which is believed, especially a system of religious
   beliefs; as, the Jewish faith
5. Complete confidence, especially in someone or something
   open to question or suspicion; certainty of goodness, reli-
   ability, skill
6. Belief that ignores or does not demand evidence; a conviction of truth
7. In an intellectual sense, belief in the existence of God;
   in a practical, religious sense, trust in God

Greek lexicons:

The noun *pistis* is akin to the Greek verb *peithō*, meaning
"to persuade." In the New Testament the word *pistis* is translated "assurance" once, "belief" once, "faith" 239 times, "fidelity" once, "them that believe" once, and "he which believeth"
once.

Pistis is:

1. Conviction of the truth of anything, belief (Plato, Josephus); in the New Testament, of a conviction or belief
   respecting man's relationship to God and divine things,
   generally with the included idea of trust and holy fervor
   born of faith and conjoined with it (e.g., 1 Co 13:13; 2 Co
   5:7; Heb 11:11).
   a) When it relates to God, *pistis* is the conviction that
      God exists and is the Creator and ruler of all things,

the provider and bestower of eternal salvation through Christ (see 1 Th 1:8; Heb 11:6; 12:2, 13:7; 1 Pe 1:21).

b) In reference to Christ, it denotes a strong and welcome conviction or belief that Jesus is the Messiah, through whom we obtain eternal salvation in the kingdom of God (see Ro 3:22; Gal 2:16, 20; Eph 3:12; Rev 14:12).

c) The religious belief of Christians:

   (1) Subjectively (Eph 4:13), a mere acknowledging of divine things and of the claims of Christianity (see Ja 2:14, 17, 20, 22, 24, 26)

   (2) Objectively, the substance of Christian faith or what is believed by Christians

d) with the predominant idea of trust (or confidence) in God or in Christ, springing from faith in the same (see Mt 8:10, 15:28; Lk 7:9, 50, 17:5)

2. Fidelity, faithfulness; that is, in the character of one who can be relied upon (see Mt 23:23; Gal 5:22; Titus 2:10)

Other sources:

The Cambridge Greek Testament has this to say about the relation between *pistis* (faith) and *erga* (works) in James 2:14-26: "Probably as a reaction from justification by works of the law, a fallacy had sprung up among the Jewish Christians that faith in Christ existing as an inactive principle, a mere speculative belief, would suffice without works. James shows what an impossible position this is. *Eleos* (compassion, mercy) is regarded as the practical result and test of *pistis* as it is in Matt. 25:35-40, a passage probably in the Apostle's mind here. The works of which St. Paul speaks are works of *pistis*, not of the Mosaic law. Such *erga* Christ Himself sets forth as required in the Christian life in the Sermon on the Mount, and in such passages as Matt. 7:20; 26:10; and others. It is noticeable also that when our Lord enjoins keeping of the commandments in Matt. 19:18-20, the instances of observances are taken from the second table, compared with this Rom 13:8. St. James' teaching here is the teaching of Christ and Paul."

Wycliffe Bible Commentary says about James 2:14-26, "This is the best known and the most widely debated passage in the epistle. These were the verses, more than any others, that caused Martin Luther to describe this book as a 'right strawy epistle.' Most of the difficulties in the interpretation of 2:14-26 have arisen out of a failure to understand that: (1) James was not refuting the Pauline doctrine of justification by faith but rather a perversion of it; (2) Paul and James used the words *works* and *justification* in different senses."

On James 2:14-26, Weiss's commentary says, "James says faith without being proved by works is useless. He is not contending against dogmatic doctrines, but he is exposing the self-deception which is found in this, that we content ourselves with mere faith. . . . Just as the charity, which finds its expression only in empty words, is of no use, if at the same time it does not bring help in need; thus, too, faith is worthless if it does not at the same time prove itself to be living by working what it should work. The mere conviction of the fact, that Jesus is our Lord (cf. 2:1), is certainly in itself alone a dead conviction, if it does not bring about the fulfilment of the will of God which has been proclaimed by Him (cf. Matt. 7:21). . . . For as the body without the soul that gives it life is dead, thus too faith is dead, if it lacks the power that produces works."

MESSAGE

To the first readers:

There is a poem, set to music, which sums up the intent of James' exhortation:

> What you are speaks so loud
> That the world can't hear what you say;
> They're looking at your walk,

Not listening to your talk;
They're judging by your actions every day.
Don't believe you'll deceive
By claiming what you've never known;
They'll accept what they see,
And know you to be;
They'll judge by your life alone.

                              MRS. H. S. LEHMAN

James and Paul are not contradictory but complementary. Each taught that faith justifies us before God, but works before men.

To modern readers:

Nothing "turns off" those of the world faster than those Christians whose faith consists only in mere profession. There is a gross misunderstanding existing among Christians today of the relationship between faith and works. James puts faith first, because faith produces works. Genuine or saving faith is always evidenced by works. Faith works. God sees our faith; the world sees our works.

SPIRIT

pneumatos—2:26

(The Saint and Service—2:14-26)

MEANING

Dictionary definitions:

Spirit refers to the breath of life; life, or the life principle; intelligent or immaterial part of man; rational soul or intellectual being not connected with the material body; disembodied soul; incorporeal being; a person's mental or moral nature or qualities (e.g., "poor in spirit").

New Testament:

Pneuma in all its forms is used 385 times and is translated as "Spirit" 133 times; "spirit" 153 times; "spiritually" twice;

"ghost" twice; "life" once; "wind" once; "Holy Spirit" with *agion* (holy) four times; "Holy Ghost" eighty-nine times. Cognates *pneumatikos* (spiritual) is used twenty-six times, and *pneumatikōs* (spiritually) is used twice.

Etymology:

The Greek noun *pneuma* is from the Greek verb *pneō*, "to breathe" (hard), or "to blow." The English word *spirit* is from the Latin *spirare*, "to breathe" or "to blow."

Greek lexicons:

1. A movement of air, breath (blast) or a breeze; the wind or the air in motion
2. The human spirit (i.e., the vital principle by which the body is animated); the rational spirit, the power by which a human being feels, thinks, wills, decides (ie., the soul); "The highest and noblest part of man, which qualifies him to lay hold of incomprehensible, invisible, eternal things" (Luther)
3. A spirit (i.e., a simple essence), devoid of all or at least of all grosser matter, and possessed of the power of knowing, desiring, deciding, and acting
   It includes:
   a) God (God is Spirit), the Holy Spirit (who can fill the lives of believers), and the spiritual nature of Christ
   b) A human soul that has left the body
   c) A spirit higher than man but lower than God (e.g., angels, demons, evil spirits
4. The disposition or influence which fills and governs the soul of anyone; the efficient source of any power; affection, emotion, desire
5. The part of man which is akin to God and serves as His instrument; the new nature of the child of God (as opposed to the "flesh")

Modern terminology:

Pneuma is the root for such words as the following:
1. Pneumatic—acting by means of wind or air
2. Pneumonia—inflammation of the lungs
3. Pneumatology—study of spiritual things, doctrine of the Holy Spirit

Summary:

The study of the spiritual realm is becoming increasingly important as parapsychology (psychical research) investigates the supernormal world of telepathy (communication by other than known physical means—thoughts, experiences, feelings, etc.) from one mind to another at a distance; clairvoyance (the power of seeing events taking place at a distance without the use of the eye); spiritism (belief in the reality of communications by various methods with disembodied spirits; mediumship (alleged state of being controlled while in a trance condition, by a disembodied spirit or spirits and of being able to receive and convey, through such control, messages from departed spirits).

The spirit in James 2:26 is that which gives life to the body, or is life to the body, enabling it to function. It is the intelligent or immaterial part of man, that by which a human being feels, thinks, wills, decides. It is the breath of God, given to man at creation, which makes him a living soul.

MESSAGE

To the first readers:

By comparison and contrast, James is showing the necessity of works in the Christian life. The comparison is at first puzzling. It would seem that faith should be compared not to the body but to the spirit, since it is a spiritual thing, whereas works are external and almost material. But James' purpose may well be as Alford says: "Faith is the body, the

sum and substance, of the Christian life; works (or obedience) is the moving and quickening of that body; just as the
spirit is the moving and quickening principle of the natural
body. So that as the body without the spirit is dead, so faith
without works is also dead."

James is stressing throughout his whole epistle that true
or living faith shall be shown by the works which will naturally accompany it, just as a living body is naturally indwelled
by a spirit. Only if faith becomes nothing more than intellectual assent to a statement of beliefs can it exist without
works, and in this condition it is more like a lifeless corpse
than a living man.

To modern readers:

While in the natural realm it is possible for faith (if it is
mere assent) to exist without works, just as it is possible for
a body to be lifeless, yet it is doubtful whether works can
effectively be present without faith, just as (without supernatural quickening) the spirit cannot exist apart from the
body. The creation of man as he is, and the doctrine of the
resurrection of the body, show that God has breathed out life
with the purpose of its being united to a body. Likewise a
moral, upright life, is to be accompanied by faith in God.
Profession of faith without practice is hollow.

TONGUE

glōssa—3:5, 6, 8

(The Saint and his Speech—3:1-12)

MEANING

Dictionary definitions:

Zondervan's Pictorial Bible Dictionary gives several definitions for the word *tongue:*

1. An organ of the body (Ps 68:23; Mk 7:33; Rev 16:10)
2. An organ of speech (Job 27:4; Ps 35:28; Mk 7:35)
3. A language or dialect (Gen 10:5, 20), translated "language" in the King James Version (Est 1:22; Dan 1:4)
4. A people or race having a common language (Is 66:18; Rev 10:11)
5. Figurative uses of the word: the tongue can be sharpened (i.e., made to utter caustic words, Ps 64:3; 140:3); it is a sharp sword (Ps 57:4); it is persuasive when it uses soft language (Pr 25:15); ranting is a rage of tongues (Ps 31:20); it is the pen of an eager writer (Ps 45:1), a shrewd antagonist (Ps 52:2); the tongue of the just is a treasure (Pr 10:20, 12:18), and a mark of wisdom (Is 50:4); it is like a bow (Jer 9:3), an arrow (Jer 9:8), and a lash (Jer 18:18); the thing that appeared at Pentecost had cloven tongues (Ac 2:3); the tongue is little but can do great things (Ja 3:5, 8); in the third chapter of James it is used as an organ of speech

New Testament:

The word *tongue* or *tongues* is used fifty-eight times: to designate a member of the body, it is used fifteen times; to designate a nation, seven times; to designate a language, speech, or word, thirty-six times as follows:

1. Once each in Mark 16:17, John 5:2, 1 Peter 3:10, and 1 John 3:18
2. Ten times in Acts
3. Twenty-two times in 1 Corinthians

The word is never used by Paul in his other epistles. In the one epistle, where it is used, 1 Corinthians, Paul writes to a carnal church (3:1) to rebuke them for the abuse of the gift.

MESSAGE

To the first readers:

Tongue is the key word in James 3:1-12. The writer enforces his teaching on a disciplined tongue by using the illustrations of the horse and the bit, the ship and the rudder, the fire and the wood, the untamed animals, the fountain and the water, and the tree and the fruit. Calvin thinks that in verse 1, James may be warning us against censorious or critical tongues that are always seeking to set other people right. This is not a manifestation of true faith—to be always criticizing others—but rather of "dead faith," for people often criticize others for the very things of which they themselves are guilty. It is more difficult to control the tongue than the actions. The size of the tongue is not the measure of its importance. James reveals that an inconsistent life is revealed by the tongue for we both bless God and curse men with the same tongue.

To modern readers:

The tongue is a restless evil, a deadly poison, endangering all who come near. It cannot be controlled by man. Man needs the Master, the Lord Jesus Christ, to master and manage this very powerful member of his body. Depraved man is not only weak; he is helpless. Meek Moses was kept out of Canaan because he spoke unadvisedly with his lips. Our Lord Jesus Christ, under much greater provocation, was led as a lamb to the slaughter and as a sheep before its shearers was dumb, so He opened not His mouth. When He was reviled, He did not retaliate but committed Himself to Him that judges righteously. In this matter of the use of the tongue, Christ is our perfect example (1 Pe 2:18-25). Our speech betrays us. On the other hand, let us remember that we may use our tongues to bless God. When thus employed, our speech is golden; when used otherwise, silence is golden.

MEEKNESS
prautēti—3:13
(The Saint and Sagacity—3:13-18)

MEANING

Dictionary definitions:

The adjective *meek* has the following shades of meaning in the English tongue:

1. Patient and mild; not inclined to anger or resentment
2. Tamely submissive; easily imposed on
3. Too submissive; spineless, spiritless
4. Gentle or kind
5. Submissive to the divine will, humility
6. Patient under injuries; longsuffering

Etymology:

Meek is from Old Norse, the word *miukr*, meaning "pliant" or "gentle." This word in turn comes from the Latin word *mucus*, meaning "slime."

Hebrew lexicons:

The Hebrew word, translated "meekness," in the Old Testament is ʿ*anavah*. This word is translated "gentleness" once; "humility" three times; "meekness" once. The adjectival from, ʿ*anav*, is translated "humble" five times; "lowly" two times; "meek" thirteen times; "poor" once. The noun ʿ*anavah*, means "humility, gentleness, condescension." The verb form ʿ*anah* means to be bowed down, to be oppressed, afflicted, maltreated. The word denotes a lowly, modest mind, which prefers to bear injuries rather than return them (see Num 12:3; Ps 9:13, 10:12, 17, 22:26, 34:2, 147:6, 149:4).

Greek lexicons:

The noun *praotēs* appears nine times in the New Testament and is translated "meekness." A similar word, *prautēs*, is used three times, twice in James (1:21; 3:13), and in 1 Peter 3:15. The adjective *praus* is used only once, Matthew 11:29. A similar adjective, *praeis*, is used three times, Matthew 5:5, 21:5; 1 Peter 3:4.

The word, as used in the New Testament, has a much deeper significance than gentleness or mildness. It is much more than a natural disposition. It is an inwrought grace of the soul, and the exercises of it are first and chiefly toward God. It is that temper of spirit in which we accept His dealing with us as good, and therefore without disputing or resisting. It is closely related to the word for *humility* and follows directly upon it (Eph 4:2). This meekness is first of all a meekness before God; however, it is exercised even before evil men, with the realization that they, with their insults and injuries, are permitted and employed by Him for the chastening and purifying of the elect. In Galatians 5:23, it is associated with self-control.

Summary:

While in English use we often associate the word *meekness* with weakness, it is never so used in the Scriptures. Gentleness is the expression of meekness. It is the opposite of self-assertiveness. It is the temper of the soul that is most like Christ Himself. He invited the weary to come to Him for rest because He was meek and lowly, and in Him they would find rest for their souls (Mt 11:28-30). Meekness is might harnessed for service. Moses in the Old Testament and Christ, in the New, are models of meekness. Moses was a leader; Christ is the Lord. Moses was "mighty in words and in deeds" among the Egyptian ruling class (Ac 7:22), yet he was only too willing to be the leader of God's people. Christ had likewise, of His own volition, placed Himself in the position of a servant, a servant to God and man; He always did those things that pleased God; and here in this world, He came not to be ministered unto, but to minister (Mt 20:28).

MESSAGE

To the first readers:

Following the discourse on man's wild tongue in chapter three, James proceeds to speak of two kinds of wisdom: the wisdom that is from above and wisdom that is earthly. The wisdom from God above is marked by purity, peace, gentleness, affability, and impartiality (3:17); but earthly wisdom breeds strife, bitterness, sensuality, envy, and every evil work. James identifies true wisdom with meekness.

To modern readers:

Considered in the light of its context in 1:21, the meek man is indeed a mighty man. It takes a strong man to keep the tongue under control and the spirit serene under duress. Only the living *Logos*, the Word of God by whom the child of God has been begotten and become a partaker of the divine nature, can produce such self-control, such mildness, such Christlikeness. We are weak; Christ is meek. Our troubled spirits become like a tempest in a teapot; Christ stills the storm.

He is a wise man who knows that he is not wise. He is a wise man, who knows that in Christ are hid all the treasures of wisdom and knowledge (Col 2:3). He is a wise man who knows that he cannot make himself clean, that it is the blood of Christ that cleanses him from all sin. He is a wise man who will yield to Christ as Lord and let Him rule without rival.

It is the absence of meekness that accounts for much of the violence among the so-called educated. The international strife, the internal struggles, the domestic divisions that threaten our homes and imperil our nation are the offspring of an educational system that has taken us further and further away from Christ, the meek but mighty Saviour. One day soon, that meek man who rode upon a colt amid cheering crowds, will come riding on the clouds of heaven to rule the earth. He is the King of kings. He is the Lord of lords.

MERCY

eleous—3:17

(The Saint and Sagacity—2:13-18)

MEANING

Dictionary definitions:

1. Forbearance from inflicting harm, especially as punishment, under provocation; compassionate treatment of an offender or adversary; compassion shown by one to another who is in his power and has no claim to kindness
2. Disposition to exercise compassion or forgiveness; willingness to spare
3. The power to be merciful
4. A blessing regarded as a manifestation of compassion
5. Compassionate treatment of the unfortunate

New Testament:

Eleos is always translated "mercy" and is used twenty-seven times. The verb form *eleō* (have mercy on, passive: obtain mercy), is used thirty-one times, and the adjective, *eleeinois* (pitiable, wretched, miserable) is used twice.

Etymology:

The Greek word *eleō* means "to pity, commiserate, have compassion on." The English comes from the French *merci*, and Latin *merces* (hire, pay, reward).

Greek lexicons:

Mercy can mean kindness; goodwill toward the miserable and afflicted, joined with a desire to relieve them.

Summary:

Mercy is the outward manifestation of pity. It assumes need on the part of him who receives it and resources adequate to meet the need on the part of the one who shows it.

When used with *peace, mercy* comes first, showing that mercy is the act of God; peace is the resulting experience in the heart of man. When used with *grace*, it comes second, showing that grace precedes mercy; that is, only the forgiven may be blessed.

Mercy in James 3:17 means "compassion and kindness shown to the needy but undeserving person." It is used in relation to the "wisdom that is from above."

MESSAGE

To the first readers:

True wisdom should be willing to submit the mind in meekness to God's influences. The resulting wisdom is pure (true and right); peaceable (not divisive); gentle (not cutting); easy to be entreated (open to other opinions and correction); full of mercy and good fruits (overflowing with feelings of compassion and kindness and expressing these feelings in actions); without partiality (steady, persistent, never wavering, accessible to all); and without hypocrisy (sincere).

To modern readers:

Every Christian needs wisdom. Natural wisdom can be divisive. Intelligent men, who know what they are talking about, may be more concerned with winning a debate or proving their own superior wisdom than they are in making new discoveries, thereby causing strife and envy.

One of the characteristics of divine wisdom is mercy. Mercy has been described as not giving a wrong person what he does deserve, whereas grace is giving him what he doesn't deserve. Mercy is a grace of God. When we come to God asking for wisdom, He never gives us what we deserve; He gives us what we ask. Mercy is compassion shown by one to another who is in his power and has no claim to kindness. The characteristics of wisdom are the qualities of Christ, who is made unto us wisdom, and in Him are hid all the treasures of true wisdom and knowledge.

PEACE

eirēnēn—3:18

(The Saint and Sagacity—3:13-18)

MEANING

Dictionary definitions:

1. A state of public tranquility or quiet; freedom from civil disturbance or agitation.

   a) The state or situation of being free from war; exemption from hostilities, especially in reference to a given nation; also, the period of such freedom from war; as, "In time of peace, prepare for war."

   b) Within a community, a state of security or order provided for by law, custom, public opinion, or the like; as, the civil guardians of the peace

2. Harmony in human or personal relations; mutual concord or amity; as, to live together in peace

3. A mutual or spiritual state in which there is freedom from that which is disquieting or disturbing, as fears, agitating passions, moral conflict; eternal repose; freedom from life's disquiet; as, "May he rest in peace"

4. Absence of noise, stir, commotion; quiet, stillness; as, the peace of the woods

5. The harmonized relationships between God and man; as, Christ is our peace (Eph 2:14)

New Testaments

The word *eirēnē* is translated "peace" eighty-eight times, "quietness" once, and "rest" once. The cognates *eirēneuō*,

George H. Thomas

"to be peaceable"; *eirēnopoieō*, "to make peace"; *eirēnikos*, "peaceable"; and *eirēnopoios*, "peacemaker" occur throughout the New Testament.

Greek lexicons:

Peace can mean:

1. A state of national tranquillity; exemption from the rage and havoc of war (Rev 6:4)
2. Peace between individuals, harmony, concord (Mt 10:34; Lk 12:51; Ac 7:26; Ro 14:17; Ja 3:18—where harmony prevails in a peaceful mind)
3. Security, safety, and prosperity (Lk 19:42; Heb 7:2)
4. The Messiah's peace (Lk 2:14)
5. The tranquil state of a soul assured of its salvation through Christ, and so fearing nothing from God; content with its earthly lot, of whatsoever sort that is (Jn 16:33; Ro 5:1, 8:6; 2 Pe 3:14)
6. The blessed state of devout and holy men after death (Ro 2:9-10).

Hebrew lexicons:

1. *Shalvah*—rest, ease, security
2. *Shalowm*—completeness, peace
3. *Damam*—to be dumb, silent
4. *Hasah*—to be or keep silent
5. *Charash*—to be silent, deaf
6. *Shalam*—to cause or make peace

Other sources:

The Cambridge Greek Testament says, regarding James 3:18: "Bitter zeal and heavenly wisdom were alike sowing seed and harvest was drawing on. But only for those who are now making peace is the fruit of righteousness being sown in peace. For the zealots whose policy was resistance and war there would be a harvest of contention and hatred.

Here too wisdom was justified by its results. Zeal came to a bitter end at the siege of Jerusalem, while the true faith of Christ won its victory of peace."

Vine's *Expository Dictionary of New Testament Words* has this comment on *eirēnē:* It describes (a) harmonious relationships between men (Matt. 10:34; Rom. 14:19); (b) between nations (Lk 14:32; Ac 12:20; Rev 6:4); (c) friendliness (Ac 15:33; 1 Co 16:11; Heb 11:31); (d) freedom from molestation (Lk 11:21, 19:42; Ac 9:31, 16:36); (e) order, in the state (Ac 24:2); in the churches (1 Co 14:33); (f) the harmonious relationships between God and man, accomplished through the gospel (Ac 10:36; Eph 2:17); (g) the sense of rest and contentment consequent thereon (Mt 10:13; Mk 5:34; Lk 1:79; 2:29; Jn 14:27; Ro 1:7, 3:17, 8:6).

Wordsworth's Greek Testament adds this comment: "This fruit is sown by them who make peace. The fruit is, as it were, contained in the seed; and they who sow the seed enjoy the fruit. 'Whatsoever a man soweth, that shall he also reap'."

Wycliffe Bible Commentary says: "This fruit of righteousness is probably best taken to mean 'the fruit which is righteousness.' This statement is in contrast with James 1:20: 'The wrath of man worketh not the righteousness of God'." This latter is achieved by peacemakers who sow in peace.

The Jamieson, Fausset, and Brown commentary has this to say about fruit that is sown: "Cf. Psalm 97:11; Isaiah 61:3, 'trees of righteousness.' Anticipatory (that is), the seed whose 'fruit,' (namely) 'righteousness,' shall be ultimately reaped, is now 'sown in peace.' 'Righteousness,' now in germ, when fully developed as fruit shall be itself the everlasting reward of the righteous. As 'sowing in peace' (cf. *'sown in dishonor,'* I Cor. 15:43) produces the 'fruit of righteousness,' so conversely 'the work' and 'effect of righteousness' is 'peace'."

Of them that make peace, this commentary continues, the word *by* implies "also that (the fruit) is for them, and to (the) good (of) them that work peace. They, and they alone, are 'blessed.' 'Peacemakers,' (are) not merely they who reconcile others, but who *work peace.* 'Cultivate peace' [Estius]. Those truly wise towards God, while peaceable and tolerant towards their neighbors, yet make it their chief concern to sow righteousness, not cloaking men's sins, but reproving them with such peaceful moderation as to be the physicians, rather than the executioners, of sinners [Calvin]."

Mayor's *Epistle of James* says that "a harvest of righteousness is the issue of the quiet and gentle ministrations of those who aim at reconciling quarrels and being themselves in peace with all men." This is the opposite of 1:20.

Lenski, in his *Epistle of James*, says that verse 18 is "an elaboration of the fruit of peace, 'peaceable' being the first great operative quality of true wisdom. Earthly wisdom and its bitter zeal and selfishness produce disturbance and every kind of bad thing (v. 15); 'fruit of the (true) righteousness is sown in peace by those making peace.' These have the true wisdom. They work to produce peace in the Christian sense, undisturbed spiritual well-being. The picture of sowing in peace is one of beautiful peace."

MESSAGE

In an age when our churches are reeking with contention and strife, when Christians spend much time worrying and fretting, and the world is full of hatred and violence, it is time that someone began to sow some peace. This is the responsibility of each consecrated Christian. But until men are changed inwardly, there will be little outward manifestation of peace.

SIN

hamartia—4:17

(The Saint and Self-will—4:13-17)

MEANING

Dictionary definitions:

Sin is transgression of the law of God; disobedience of the

divine will; moral failure, especially as religiously interpreted, as contrary to the will of God; failure to realize the moral ideal in conduct and character, at least as fully as possible under existing circumstances; failure to do as one might toward one's fellowman. In general, sin is an offence; a violation of property; a misdemeanor.

Use in the New Testament:

Hamartia is translated "sin" 172 times; "offence" once; "sinful" once. Its cognate *hamartēma* is translated "sin" four times; *hamartanō*, ("sin," verb), thirty-nine times; *hamartōlos*, "sinful" four times and "sinner" forty-three times.

Similar words: *asebeia* ("ungodliness," meaning "impiety") seventeen times; *parakoē* ("disobedience to a voice") three times; *anomia* ("contempt and violation of law, lawlessness, transgression, iniquity") twenty-eight times; *parabasis* ("transgression") sixteen times; *paraptōma* ("offence, trespass, sin") twenty-three times; *agnoēma* ("error," out of ignorance) once; *hettēma* "fault," failing when one should have stood) four times; *adikia* ("unrighteousness") sixty-seven times; *ponēria* ("depravity, wickedness, evil") eighty-five times; *epithumia* ("lust, desire for what is forbidden") fifty-four times.

Greek lexicons:

In classical Greek, the verb *hamartanō* was used with reference to archery, to mean "miss the mark." As used in the New Testament, it has these shades of meaning:

1. A failing to hit the mark; a sinning, whether by omission or commission, in thought and feeling, or in speech and action; error
2. A sin; that which is done wrong, committed or resultant sin; an offence; a violation of the divine law in thought or in action; a bad action; evil deed

3. Collectively, the complete or aggregate of sins committed by a single person or by many
4. A principle or cause of sin; an error of the understanding
5. A proneness to sin, sinful propensity
6. A guilty subject, sin offering, expiatory victim

Summary:

The word *sin* may be a principle or source of action, or an inward element producing acts. It is a governing principle or power, leading to a sinful deed, or an act of sin.

Sin is voluntary, ethical, hence never necessarily inherent in man's physical or finite nature.

It is the refusal to be guided in life by the restraining and directing influence of the knowledge of God's power (Ro 1:18, 28), of His nature (Jn 3:19), and of His love revealed in His Son (Jn 3:36). Such a knowledge of God comes to all men from their nature (Ro 2:14-15), from creation (Ro 1:20), and from the Spirit of God (Jn 1:9).

Transgression of known law, then, is sin; but so is wrong attitude, wrong desire, wrong "set" of the will or self. Thus, sin is unbelief (Heb 3:12, 19), the centering of the self upon something, or someone, less than God Himself.

Sin is not an entity, neither a material nor a spiritual substance. Sin is any attitude of indifference, unbelief, or disobedience to the will of God revealed in conscience, law, or gospel—whether this attitude expresses itself in thought, word, deed, or settled disposition and conduct.

MESSAGE

To the first readers:

In the context of James 4:13-17, sin is the neglect of doing what one knows to be the good, the godly thing to do. This negligence amounts to a deliberate refusal to act up to a recognized standard. The essence of sin is self-will. This is a vital aspect of personality. The sin comes in exercising this will in a way that either ignores God or rejects Him. It is not a sin to plan one's future, but it is a sin to plan that future without reference to God.

To set one's heart on earthly gain and gold, to live for the here and now, is sin. The careless chatter of those who say, "Let us eat, drink, and be merry; for tomorrow we die," is sin. To live on the horizontal plain only, with no reference to God on the vertical plain, is sin. In fact, James goes on to show in the verses that follow in chapter five, that that kind of thinking will dominate in the last days before Christ's return. In that way men nourish their souls for the slaughter.

To modern readers:

Sin is the refusal to be guided in life by God. It is therefore a refusal to be guided by the light that comes to man in creation, conscience, history, and in the Lord Jesus Christ and His Word. Sin is the centering of self upon someone, or something other than God Himself. It is an attitude as well as an act. It can be an attitude of indifference, unbelief, or disobedience, whether expressed in thought, word, deed, disposition, or conduct. Sin, as was the original fall of man, is usually first in imagination and affection and thought, and then in deed. It is choosing to center one's life about one's own purposes, rather than making God the center and goal.

Horizontal living is not limited to the folk living on this continent. Many spend exorbitant sums in sinful dissipation. Others are losing their lives while making a living, like Elimelech in the book of Ruth. It requires a divine miracle to free a man from the love of the world and to create in him a love for God and neighbor that transcends all other loves. God is abundantly able to work this miracle in one's life, if one will only seek and see.

SICKNESS
(*asthenei, kamnonta*–5:14-15)
(The Saint and Sickness–5:13-20)

MEANING

Dictionary definitions:

Webster's Dictionary defines *sick* as meaning "either affected with disease; not well or healthy in a physical sense; spiritually or morally unsound or corrupt; mentally or emotionally unsound or disordered; affected in a psychological sense or by some strong emotion."

Etymology:

The word in English is traced back to the Middle English, *sik, sek*; the old Norse *sykks* ("sick or distressed"), and the Middle Irish *socht* ("depression or silence").

Hebrew lexicons:

Hebrew words for *sick* mainly implied the physical disease or illness when translated as *sick*, such as, *'anash* and *tachalu'*. The most common form, *chalah* (used in this manner in Gen 48:1; 2 Ch 32:24), was also used for psychological depression or weakness (e.g., 2 Sa 13:2; Pr 13:12).

Greek lexicons:

In the New Testament, various Greek words are used for *sick*, and quite often these have overlapping meanings. *Arrōstos* ("not robust or strong") is used in Matthew 14:14; Mark 6:5, 13; and 1 Corinthians 11:30. *Echō kakos* ("to be ill") could quite easily imply the sickness of the mind and of the soul as well (e.g., Mt 4:24; Mt 9:12; Lk 7:2). The verb *astheneō* (used in Ja 5:14, and thirty-six times in the New Testament) has been translated as follows: "be diseased, be made weak, be sick, be weak, be impotent." The noun *asthenēs* (used twenty-four times) is translated as follows: "feeble, impotent, sick, weak, without strength, sick folks, weakness, weak things." The verb *kamnō* (Ja 5:15) has been translated: "be wearied, faint," and in its participial form in our text, "sick."

In the classical Greek from the time of Euripides, *astheneō* has been used for "weak, feeble, to be without strength, powerless." It is used in Romans 8:3 to refer to the impotence of the law because of the weakness of the flesh. It is used for contrast in 2 Corinthians 12:10, which says (paraphrased), "When I am weak in human strength, then am I strong in strength divine." In the dative it implies a weakness in faith and convictions about lawful things (e.g., 1 Co 8:9). In James 5:14, it means "weak, needy, or poor, especially a debility of health."

Its cognate *asthenēs* is the root of our English word *asthenia*, meaning "a lack or loss of strength; debility, deficient vitality." It is used to mean "without strength, infirm" (Mt 25:39, 43, 44). It is used most often as "weak" (thirteen times). It is used to refer to physical weakness (Mt 26:41); as a judgment upon spiritual laxity in a church (1 Co 11:30); for comparative degrees of weakness (1 Pe 3:7). In a spiritual sense, it is used of the rudiments of the Jewish religion in its inability to justify anyone (Gal 4:9); to be weak morally or ethically (1 Co 8:7); rhetorically of God's actions, according to the human estimate (1 Co 1:25).

The verb *kamnō* from which comes the participle *kamnonta*, in James 5:15, means "to labor, and thus to suffer from fatigue." It is used three times in the New Testament, translated in the King James as "be wearied" (Heb 12:3); "sick" (Ja 5:15); and "fainted" (Rev 2:3). It is used in the Septuagint in Job 10:1 and 17:2.

According to Vine, it means "primarily, to work, hence from the effect of constant work, to be weary e.g. James 5:15; Heb. 12:3."

Summary:

With regard to the distinction between the two words, *asthenei* and *kamnonta*, Vine says, "The choice of this verb instead of the repetition of *asthenō* is suggestive of the common accompaniment of sickness, weariness of mind, which not infrequently hinders physical recovery; hence this special cause is here intimated in the general idea of sickness."

MESSAGE

To the first readers:

James instructs the one who is sick, too weak to walk to a public service, too weak to rise from his bed, too weary with labor to help himself or to call for help. He is to call to his bedside the elders of the church. James assumes that there are elders, that they are known as such, and that there is a recognized assembly to which this brother belongs. The call comes from the one who is sick, not from any preacher summoning the sick to come forward in a public service. The call goes to the elders, whose qualifications are clearly set forth in 1 Timothy 3:1-7 and Titus 1:5-9. The elders are to begin to supplicate, to pray earnestly, to pray fervently, to empathize with the one who is sick, to anoint him with oil in the name of the Lord, to believe that God will raise him up from the sick bed and strengthen him. If the sick person has sinned and is in a state of sin, this hindrance can be removed, the sin forgiven, dismissed.

The hindrance to an answer may lie with the elders, who may need to confess their own sins openly to one another (5:16). The hindrance may lie with the church, the body of Christ. One sick member can affect the whole body, the whole local assembly. However, a sick person may spark a revival in a church, and that revival could start in the place of human infirmity, where a person lies helpless and wants to implore divine intervention. If the prayer of one righteous person, Elijah, could bring such a miraculous answer, what would result from a church thoroughly getting right with God?

If a man, being a brother in Christ, wanders from the path, then let everyone pray and work for his restoration. When an erring brother is returned, a person can be saved from physical death or spiritual death, and a multitude of sins that would otherwise be committed, will be avoided.

To modern readers:

The message in this passage does not lend support to the much publicized healing services of today, where attention is directed to some self-acclaimed faith healer. Neither does our text lend any support to the teachings of the Roman Catholic church on extreme unction. The passage directs attention to the God who answers prayer when certain conditions are met. Faith in God works wonders.

When a church is sick spiritually, then answers to prayer are rare. When a church is in robust health, when the saints are right with God and with one another, miracles in answer to prayer are the rule, not the exception. Sickness in any member of the church should be regarded as a call to trust God to effect a recovery. To them that have no might, He increases strength. And they that wait upon the Lord shall have their strength renewed (Is 40:31).

PRAYER
euchomai, proseuchomai, erotaō, and *deomai*
(The Saint and Sickness—5:13-20)

MEANING

James 5:13-20 contains one of the most referred-to passages on healing. Yet taken as a whole, this passage emphasizes more than healing; namely, prayer.

Greek lexicons:

There are four Greek words for the verb "pray":

1. *Euchomai* means "to pray or to wish."
2. *Proseuchomai* means "to pray to God" and is used only in this sense.
3. *Erotaō* means "to ask or to make request."
4. *Deomai* means "to desire or beseech."

There are also four words for "prayer":

1. *Euchē* denotes a prayer or a vow, such as Paul took when he was going to Jerusalem.
2. *Proseuchē* is used of prayer in general with emphasis on the element of devotion.
3. *Deēsis* stresses the idea of personal need in prayer.
4. *Enteuzis*, the rarest of the four, used only in 1 Timothy 2:1 and 4:5, is the term used on papyri to denote a petition to a superior; in the New Testament it has the connotation of approaching God with childlike confidence and conversing with Him.

Use in James:

James uses the words *proseuchomai, euchomai, euchē,* and *deēsis.* Let us narrow our scope of enquiry to these four words.

1. *Proseuchomai* is by far the most commonly used word for prayer in the New Testament, used in the synoptics and Acts, but not in John.
2. *Euchomai*, on the other hand, is the rarest word used for praying. It is used more with the idea of "wish" (e.g., Ac 26:29, "I would to God—"). It also appears in Acts 27:29 in the description of the storm. "They . . . wished for the day."
3. *Euchē* is one of the rarest nouns for "prayer." It means "prayer or vow." It is used in the Septuagint to denote consecration. It appears only three times in the New Testament (Ac 18:18, 21:23; Ja 5:16).
4. *Deēsis* is "primarily a wanting, a need, an asking, entreaty,

supplication." It does not always apply to prayer but may be used with reference to a request from one man to another. Typical of the use of *deēsis* are passages such as Luke 5:33, Romans 10:1, and 2 Timothy 1:3.

Examination of context:

In verse thirteen, those who are afflicted are exhorted to pray. *Proseuchesthō* is a present imperative, third person, singular. In the English we do not have third person imperative forms and consequently must translate, "Let him pray." This is weak; in the Greek it is a command.

Similarly, a third person, plural, imperative verb, *proseuzasthōsan*, is used in verse fourteen commanding the elders to pray for the sick. In verse thirteen, the verb is in the present tense, but in verse 14 it is in the aorist tense (likely an ingressive aorist). This suggests that the person who is afflicted is to pray and to keep on praying. However, the elders are to pray at a particular point of time to meet a particular crisis.

In verse fifteen, *euchē tēs pisteos* is translated "the prayer of faith." In the Septaugint, this word means "consecration." One might interpret this as meaning that the elders consecrate or dedicate the sick person (i.e., in effect they say, "God, he is in Your hands"). Consecration seems to imply a ritual. Here the elders anoint with oil. James does not here advocate ritual for ritual's sake. Notice that he qualifies it, "the consecration of faith." Thus when the elders anoint the sick man with oil, they are symbolically attesting to their faith in God's ability to heal. The act of anointing is of little worth in itself, but it demonstrates faith. Those who use this method are saying, "God, since You have asked us to anoint the sick, the very fact that we do it means that we believe in Your power to heal." Otherwise it would be senseless.

In verse 16 we are commanded to pray for one another. This is another imperative. This time, however, it is a different verb (*euchesthe*) which connotes wishing or desiring. We should try to empathize with the party for whom we are praying. We ought to pray as if his needs were our own, and not just rattle off a list of requests in a perfunctory manner.

In verse 16, we are told "the effectual fervent prayer of a righteous man availeth much." *Ischuei deēsis*, translated "effectual fervent prayer" means literally "a prayer of strength." The emphasis here is on personal need. If a righteous man asks persistently, unwaveringly, in great earnestness, not weakening in his faith, his prayer will not be fruitless.

Verse 17 tells us that Elijah was only human. Yet when he "prayed earnestly" it stopped raining for three years and six months. "Prayed earnestly" is used to translate *proseuchei proseuzato* which means literally "prayed a prayer." Vine says this is a Hebraistic idiom. The effectiveness of prayer is again brought out in verse eighteen.

MESSAGE

Taken as a whole, the passage teaches us the great value of prayer. The sick are to begin praying habitually. The elders are to pray at a particular time of crisis, and they are to expect an answer. Prayer is to be accompanied by faith and obedience. We are to empathize with those for whom we pray. At times there must be persistent, persevering, prevailing prayer. God is sovereign in nature and in this whole wide world, as well as in the confines of a sickroom.

BIBLIOGRAPHY

Arndt, William F., and Gingrich, F. Wilbur. *A Greek-English Lexicon of the New Testament.* Chicago: U. of Chicago, 1957.

Buttrick, George Arthur, ed. *The Interpreter's Bible.* Vol. 12. New York: Abingdon-Cokesbury, 1957.

Cremer, Herman. *Biblico-Theological Lexicon of New Testament Greek.* Edinburgh: T. & T. Clark, 1895.

Englishman's Greek Concordance of the New Testament. 9th ed. London: Samuel Bagster & Sons, 1903.

Gesenius, William. *Hebrew and English Lexicon.* Trans. Edward Robinson. Boston: Crocker & Brewster, 1863.

Gibson, E. C. S. "St. James." In *The Pulpit Commentary,* ed. H. D. M. Spence and Excell, J. S., vol. 49. New York: Funk & Wagnalls, n.d.

Jamieson, Robert; Fausset, A. R.; and Brown, David. *Commentary Practical on the Whole Bible.* Grand Rapids: Zondervan, n.d.

Kittel, Gerhard, ed. *Theological Dictionary of the New Testament.* Vols. 1-5. Trans. and ed. by Geoffrey W. Bromiley. Grand Rapids: Eerdmans, 1964-67.

Lange, John Peter. *A Commentary on the Holy Scriptures.* Vol. 23. Trans. and ed. with additions, by Philip Schaff. Grand Rapids: Zondervan, n.d.

Lenski, Richard Charles Henry. *The Interpretation of the Epistle to the Hebrews and of the Epistle of James.* Columbus, O.: Wartburg, 1946.

Liddell, Henry George, and Scott, Robert. *A Greek-English Lexicon.* 2 vols. 1843. Reprint. Oxford: Clarendon, 1953.

Maclaren, Alexander. *Expositions of Holy Scripture.* Vol. 15. Grand Rapids, Eerdmans, 1944.

Mayor, Joseph B. *The Epistle of James.* Rev. ed. Grand Rapids: Zondervan, 1954.

Moulton, James Hope, and Milligan, George. *The Vocabulary of the Greek New Testament.* London: Hodder and Stoughton, 1952.

Pfeiffer, Charles F., and Harrison, Everett F., eds. *Wycliffe Bible Commentary.* Chicago: Moody, 1962.

Plummer, Alfred. "A Critical and Exegetical Commentary on the Epistle of James." In *The International Critical Commentary.* 1916. Reprint. Edinburgh: T. & T. Clark, 1954.

Plumptre, E. H. *The General Epistle of St. James.* Cambridge Bible for Schools and Colleges. London: Cambridge U., 1882.

Robertson, Archibald Thomas. *Word Pictures in the New Testament.* Vol. 6. Nashville: Broadman, n.d.

Scrivener, Frederick Henry Ambrose. *The New Testament in the Original Greek.* London: Cambridge U., 1881.

Tenney, Merrill C. *The New Testament: An Historical and Analytic Survey.* 2d ed. Grand Rapids: Eerdmans, 1954.

———, ed. *Zondervan's Pictorial Bible Dictionary.* Grand Rapids: Zondervan, 1963.

Thayer, Joseph Henry. *A Greek-English Lexicon of the New Testament.* New York: Amer. Book, 1889.

Thiessen, Henry Clarence. *Introduction to the New Testament.* Grand Rapids: Eerdmans, 1950.

Vincent, Marvin R. *Word Studies in the New Testament.* Vol. 1. Grand Rapids: Eerdmans, 1946.

Vine, W. E. *An Expository Dictionary of New Testament Words.* Vols. 1-4. London: Oliphants, 1940-48.

Weiss, Bernhard. *Commentary on the New Testament.* 4 vols. Trans. W. G. H. Schodde and E. Wilson. New York: Funk & Wagnalls, 1906.

Wordsworth, Christopher. *The New Testament of Our Lord and Saviour Jesus Christ.* Vol. 2. London: Gilbert & Rivington, 1889.

Wuest, Kenneth. *Word Studies in the Greek New Testament.* Vols. 1-4. Fincastle, Virginia: Scripture Truth, 1944-54.

Young, Robert. *Analytical Concordance to the Bible.* New York: Funk & Wagnalls, n.d.